Romance 101 for Men

Romance 101 for Men

Recipes for the Game of Love

Randy J. Hartman, M.A.

Writers Club Press
San Jose New York Lincoln Shanghai

Romance 101 for Men
Recipes for the Game of Love

Writers Club Press
an imprint of iUniverse.com, Inc.

For information address:
iUniverse.com, Inc.
620 North 48th Street, Suite 201
Lincoln, NE 68504-3467
www.iuniverse.com

ISBN: 0-595-13128-X

Printed in the United States of America

CONTENTS

INTRODUCTION

First and foremost I want to thank you for your interest in this book. That speaks well of your romantic interests in life! Romance is for everyone. No one is excluded unless they chose to exclude themselves from the gift of love and romance. Love is such a beautiful and fragile gift that we give to one another from our hearts, but sometimes with the passing years of life and the problems that go along with life, we sometimes push our feelings of love and romance to the back of our minds and hearts. It is truly a shame that society and the stresses of daily life allow us to become jaded.

There are currently numerous books on the market that attempt to address the art of romance, but unfortunately none of them seems to provide a workable blueprint that guys can follow! Yes, we guys need to fess up to the fact that most of us are romantically impaired. I believe that it is something in our social roles here in America that impedes the romantic growth of males. Other societies encourage males to be loving and romantic starting at an early age. In our school system we could use a mandatory course for males in Romance 101 or Loving for Beginners.

It can be difficult at times to even think in romantic terms with the stress of work and all the other expectations society has put upon us. I have also suffered through those times of stress and that became one of my main motivations to put together this love recipe book for men. The idea of using the format of a cookbook came to me one day while I was still in the "thinking" stages of this book. As a man, I knew other men like myself need clear step-by-step instructions to successfully put together any type of a real romantic interlude. What better than a cookbook! All the necessary ingredients are listed first, then followed by easy step-by-step instructions that are man-proof!

This book will have a good smattering of food recipes. Food is also an important part of the sensuality of romance. Many of my love recipes have incorporated the use of food products that stimulate an individual's own sense of sensuality. Keep in mind that the term "sensual" implies all of our senses, not just the sense of physical touch. We also need to include the senses of smell, taste, sight and hearing. This is why I have found it necessary to include some very simple, but wonderful little food dishes that can be easily whipped up with the minimum amount of time and effort. A small array of these foods to enjoy sets the stage for romance in the first degree! In the area of romance and seduction there is no room for calorie counting, only room for indulging in the wonderful world of food and romance!

Why would anyone want to continue to deprive themselves of all the beauty and splendor that accompanies romance? I would encourage you to use this book as a springboard to fanning your flames of romance. Every recipe in this book is very flexible. Feel free to adjust and mix and match as your romantic spirit moves you. With any luck your love could move from the warm embers to the white hot passion that once was experienced earlier in your relationship, or ignite the flames of a very new and promising romance.

Go for the gusto and your rewards will be abundant and will come back to you in many splendid ways!

INSTRUCTIONS FOR THE ROMANTICALLY CHALLENGED MALE

Hey guys, don't lose hope forever of becoming a romantic, it can happen to you too. For more years than I can image, or would even want to guess, women have pinned this bad rap on us as animals with no type of romantic sensitivity. Now is the time for the brotherhood to stand up and be counted and recognized as people with feeling too. Sure, sometimes we screw it up real bad with a lack of sensitivity and no emphases on feelings, but we really have it within ourselves to be romantic! (Even romantic in the truest sense of the word, from emotional to caring and even gentle at times.)

In Dr John Grey's book, *Men are from Mars, Women are from Venus*, he really hit the proverbial nail on the head. We men are guilty of wanting to retreat to our caves to regroup and settle down from our day of being the hunter. Being in the hunter role will take a lot out of a fellow during the course of the day. We need to try and see things and feel things like our lovers do, and believe you me it is not easy!

Men, we need to first define what romance is to the female being. Believe me when I say it is not just a roll in the hay! While romance may lead to sex, it does not start out as a sexual quest for the female. Only if she feels you have earned and deserve sex will you receive it. Don't get to cocky dude, she can take away as well as give! There is an old adage that seems so true to me, "The hand that rocks the cradle rules the world." What most females seem to want is for their man to be caring and do caring things for them, and willing to focus some of their time on them.

Now that really does not seem so hard, or is it? It is difficult at times to unwrap and decompress from our daily concerns and worries to focus on another person in a caring and loving way. If we think back in time to when we first got involved in this relationship with our special someone, honestly, what was our behavior then? If the truth were known, most of us guys were loving, caring and attentive to our honey bunnies. In the beginning there were some white hot flashes of romances going on within us! I guess the question now is, can we fan those flames again and breathe a strong sense of romance and passion back into our lives?

All things are possible if we really want them. After we get what we want we get lost in the day to day struggles that we as hunters must face. It is sad that we usually do not consider change or find the motivation to change until we are faced with a crisis.

Being romantic can be a lot of fun and really make us feel good about ourselves. The romantic recipes in this book are only a simple guide to follow to just help you get that "jump start" back to romance in your life. I would encourage you to start by finding an interesting theme in one of these recipes and use it, modify it, bend it, do whatever it takes to make it fit for you. With your first romantic endeavor you can expect your lover to maybe wonder what is up with you and why are you doing this. By your second romantic adventure you can bet she will probably be totally receptive to your advances.

Romance can be found in so many different ways. Some times romance can be found in some thing as simply as you preparing a simple meal or snack, and then sharing it with her in a caring way. Remember, whatever attitude we put out into the world will always come right back at us, ouch! A loving and caring attitude can reawaken our love, give us peace and even lower our blood pressure!

I have heard it said over the years that the journey of a thousand miles begins with the first step. Are you ready to take that first step, and then keep putting one romantic foot in front of the other?

Balloons Galore!

20+balloons, assorted colors

String ribbon

Black indelible marker

A strong sense of passion

Balloons are extremely versatile in sending messages to your loved one. In this endeavor I would recommend that you blow up/ inflate 20 or more balloons in assorted colors. You can purchase these balloons already filled with helium or simply inflate them yourself. Unless you have very strong lungs I would recommend than you spend a few extra dollars at the craft store and purchase a hand pump for balloons. You can make this as fancy or as simple as you chose to. The string ribbon is for tying a tail on each balloon for easier handling.

Once you have all the balloons inflated, the really challenging part starts with you writing romantic and loving messages on each balloon! Try using one word or up to one sentence. Use whatever seems to work for you, You might want to consult the dictionary. Good examples would be: "I love you", "Thinking of you", "Your love fuels my fire". You may want to think ahead and write down on paper numerous possibilities for these love notes that you will put on the balloons.

It is important to remember to use an indelible marker to write on the balloons. Any other types of markers will smear very easily and destroy your messages of love.

Now what? You could fill her car with balloons, have them delivered to her office, fill the bed with balloons. Let us see how creative your romantic side can be!

FLOWERS FOR MY LOVE

Bouquet of flowers

Crystal flower vase

Attractive stationary

Flowers for your love-it's almost a tradition in American society. With this approach you will need to exercise your best romantic side to pull this off.

With some very attractive stationary you will be writing a love note to go with the flowers. This is a more unique approach to a love note as you need to speak to each type and color of flower in the bouquet, so pick your bouquet carefully!

I offer these examples to better illustrate my point. With a red tulip I might add to the love note " The petals of the red tulip are so soft and beckoning as your sweet lips" and "The white rose speaks of the purity and tenderness of my love for you". "The yellow daffodil signifies how my heart springs forward into the sunshine every time you walk into the room".

As I said earlier, choose your flower bouquet very carefully, but I strongly encourage you to use four or more different flowers in your arrangement. Your love note should fill up almost a full page of stationary.

INDULGING THE FIVE SENSES

A mixture of things that:

Smell good

Taste good

Feel good

Look good

Sounds good

Blindfold

From the list of ingredients it's pretty easy to see where this recipe is going! The average person has five senses: smell, taste, physical feelings, sight and sound. This could bring about a wonderful array of creative possibilities.

Start by blindfolding your partner and then slowly indulge her senses, one sensory system at a time. You might consider using a feather, a piece of chocolate, whipped cream, strawberries, scented candles, or very romantic background music. This can be as sensual or sexy as you want to make it! Of course, may sure that you will have quality uninterrupted time to indulge your lover. You owe it to yourselves to enjoy a few of life's little pleasures! Just open your mind up to all the wonderful possibilities.

DINNER THEATER SPECIAL

Dinner theater reservations for two

Formal/semi-formal attire

This is a golden opportunity to wine and dine your special lover. Most women always seem to enjoy a formal/semi-formal evening out, especially if you suggest it. Hey guys, it really doesn't hurt us to get a little dressed up once in a while, and the fringe benefits can be fantastic!

Simply start with making reservations at a local dinner theater for a Friday or Saturday evening. Of course try to find a theater with an interesting show! For your lady, try to consider a musical, romantic or a comedy. The new wave of interactive plays where the audience gets actually involved in the play. It is always good to inform your love of the pending plans. Don't be hesitate to dress up for the evening to show her how much you care. You can bet she will be greatly appreciative of your effort. For the evening you can expect to enjoy a quiet dinner chatting with your love and then when you are still at your table you will be entertained with a live show.

Anytime you can make your love feel like a special lady, you can be sure that you will reap spectacular rewards for your effort!

THE ROAD TO HEAVEN IS LINED WITH ROSES

Four dozen plus Roses

Chocolate

Wine (or beverage of your choice)

Over the years roses have been always known as a symbol of love. Symbolism in the expression of love has always been well accepted and appreciated in nearly all cultures, and nothing says it better than diamonds and roses. I would venture a guess that if you are like the rest of us working people you probably also find that roses are more affordable.

The idea I propose here is a simple one: Send her roses! The different twist here is to send different color roses on different days. You will need to check with your local florist to see what colors are typically available in your area.

As an example I offer the following scenario. Four days before our wedding anniversary I arranged with the florist to deliver my wife roses. One dozen pink roses on Wednesday, one dozen white roses on Thursday, one dozen yellow roses on Friday. For our anniversary on Saturday they delivered one dozen red roses.

Depending on the cost of the roses and colors available, you could tailor this idea to fit your needs. To add more glamour you could also have chocolates and wine delivered with the roses.

LOVING HER AT WORK

Twelve roses

Restaurant reservations

Love is in the air everywhere, and the workplace is no exception. Sending flowers, roses or otherwise to your love at her work site makes her feel proud and the other women in the office very envious!

The simplicity of this plan alone makes it a very do-able recipe. A little planning must be done ahead of time. A working example might be if you sent your lover a beautiful bouquet of flowers to her office with a brief note or card. The note could speak of your great love for her and ask her to meet you for lunch at an appointed time and place.

From the lunch meeting joint plans can be drawn up for a festive evening of love! A mid-week day is always exceptionally good timing for the work weary lady in your life!

This would also be a good recipe to combine with some other evening type recipes in this book. Remember to be creative and try to see the world around you through the eyes of your loved one.

The rewards you will reap will surely be far worth the effort you put into this recipe!

THE SPECIAL GREETING CARD

Water colors

Markers

A very tall piece of cardboard

Pictures, photos

Dried flowers

Crayons

This greeting of card can be for any occasion, or no particular occasion other that to say "I love you" or "I am thinking of you". The first thing to find is a very large piece of cardboard to work with. I like the tri-fold cardboard that you can find at office supply stores that are typically used for business type presentations. Normally they have a white surface on one side and a brown surface on the reverse surface.

You can decorate your card in various ways; let your romantic love light burn brightly as you start making plans to decorate this card. Other than writing or drawing on the card, you may want to consider using some photos or pictures cut out from magazines to convey your message. Something like plastic or dried flowers could be attached.

THE FIRST KISS

The location of your first kiss

Something symbolic of the place you first kissed.

Type of flowers, drink, music from the event of the first kiss

"The first kiss". Just those three words resonate of romance! To see if this concept will even work for you and your lover, you first need to review in your memory the place and circumstances of that first kiss. Depending on the circumstances and location you may not be able to recreate the first kiss.

If the concept of recreating that first kiss seems reasonable to do, go for it! A good approach might be to leave your lover a note, on the front door, the steering wheel of the car, etc, that instructs her to meet you at that special place! Wherever your special place may be, you might need to go there in advance to ensure that the scene is set properly. I would urge you to spare nothing or overlook anything in your preparation for this event.

The reenactment of the first kiss is only the beginning. Continue to bring back alive the events and passion that followed that first kiss. If you risk nothing, you receive nothing in return.

HEAVENLY WATER

Bubble bath

Roses

Votive candles with holders

Red sweet wine (or beverage of your choice)

Incense of your choice

Ambiance is everything…this scenario does live up to its name! The best place to start is to see if your lover is up for the idea of "wet" romance. Some people cannot stand to have another person in the bathroom with them!

The starting point is to prepare the candles. There are a wide variety of candles on the market, but I would recommend about a dozen or so votive candles. Consider also adding incense if your lover likes a special scent. Once you have drawn the bath water you also have a few more options to consider. With the bath water you could use bubble bath soap, or my favorite, which is to remove the petals from a rose and scatter them in the water. If available, scented herbal soap would be a nice touch.

Depending upon your individual preferences you may consider pouring two glasses of wine. I would suggest a sweet red wine or the beverage of your choice. Don't forget to layout the wash cloths and towels! Remember to turn the music down low before you and your lover get into the tub. Depending on the tub you might be able to sit face to face, but most people seem to prefer sitting behind their lover, leaving her accessible to your touch and romantic whispers. Remember that you are only limited by your imagination for these romantic and erotic interludes!

How Many Ways Do I Love Thee?

One Pen

One pad of paper

Wine (or other beverage)

Music

This particular recipe is designed as a couple's game. It has been said that love is truly a game of life, and not for the faint of heart. Somewhere in our classic writings I recall the verse, "How many ways do I love thee, let me count the ways".

It is from that statement that the ground rules are set. As in most cases you need to ensure that the two of you have your privacy. Then I recommend that you both retire to your love chamber to start the game. After you both get as comfortable/undressed as you want to be, you are ready to go.

You each need to take turns telling each other "How do I love thee"? No mirroring or repeating what the other person has said. You keep going back and forth until one person cannot think of anything to say within one minute.

The losing partner agrees to fulfill his or her winning partner's request. How many ways do you love your partner?

Winter Picnic Lunch

Vehicle

Table cloth

Assorted food

Beverage(s)

Mood music

There are a good number of variations that you can employ with this picnic lunch scenario depending on the weather and situation. Just the idea of having a picnic with your loved one can be a romantic thing all by itself! This is a wonderful opportunity to spend time together and plan an intimate rendezvous in the next few hours. Possibly your picnic location may provide you the opportunity to go from a romantic time to an intimate encounter in the same location!

Picnics are usually a summertime activity, but picnics can still be done in the wintertime. I would like to offer the following example as an inclement weather picnic. Arrange to meet with your lover in a vehicle (with a working heater) for your winter picnic. Now spread your tablecloth in the front seat or center console. Carefully set your lunch out on the tablecloth. A wonderful suggestion would be smoked salmon, crab dip with crackers and a sandwich. The beverage of choice could range from soda to sparkling cider. Now the mood can be completed with a little music in the background. So now the stage is set for a little romance and intimate conversation. Planning for that intimate encounter later in the day can be very stimulating. What a great way to beat those winter time blues!

THE LONGEST LOVE LETTER IN HISTORY

Ink Pen

Writing tablet

Romantic inspirations

Relaxed frame of Mind

Patience and romantic are the key elements in this extreme recipe for love. At the very least, this exercise will help you wake up the romantic that has been sleeping in you! For many people the problem with doing this is just getting started.

I would like to suggest that you start with pen in hand, in a very quiet environment where you can concentrate and search your memory easily. You could consider starting your letter with talking about the things in your partner that first caught your interest, or maybe your first kiss. From that jumping off point you could go in several directions. Adding some poetry from another book could be a nice touch if you use the poetry wisely. Do not choose a long poem to just fill up space, or use more than two published poems. If you can craft a few poems of your own that would be great!

You could write about the other person's qualities of love. Talk about their eyes, their hair, lips, body, and demeanor. Let your thoughts of your lover ride on the wings of your caring and loving heart. For some of us to write like this can seem like an unnatural act, but love can carry us to our destination.

Cool Love

Ice, cracked or cubed

Ice cream alternative

Almost everyone I have spoke to thinks loving is cool, but this cool love is literally on the cold side! As with so many of these love recipes you need to ensure that your lover is primed for lingering eroticism.

This type of pleasuring involves the use of ice! The ice can be any type you prefer, cubed, crushed or cracked. Basically this is done mostly as foreplay activity. Simply take the ice into your mouth and begin foreplay, start with long deep kissing and work your cold tongue down her neck and around the back. When you get to her nipples take a little more time there. Usually you can expect her nipples to become very erect and hard as they react to the cold stimuli. From there continue downwards on your quest replenishing your mouth with ice often. Don't forget to lavish your attention on her belly button as you continue down to the inside of her thighs. Continue your journey to all the wonderful places she desires your touch.

The eroticism is great for all involved, especially if you take time to linger in all of her "special" places. Cool love is for cool people who really dare to enjoy some of life's true pleasures. Do you dare to rise to the occasion?

CHOCOLATE DELIGHT

Chocolate, solid or liquid
(Your preference)

Chocolate is truly the food of love, and is so versatile in loving ways! In this recipe for chocolate delight your sweet tooth will also be satisfied. With a little experimenting you can find out which type of chocolate will work best for you. Some possibilities are using pieces of dark chocolate, or my favorite, Magic Shell chocolate.

With the romantic mood set and your lover's motor running, you can take the selected chocolate and trace it all over her body, going for all those special places that are sure to please her. Another slant on this would be to give her the chocolate and let her trace it all over her body. This will also help you clearly identify all of her pleasure points! This will also be a great bonus for your future knowledge and pleasuring.

It is important that you make a clean lick of it! (Yes, the pun was intended) Go after all that chocolate like it's your last meal! Another tip is that magic shell chocolate also comes in a strawberry flavor, but the partial drawback to using magic shell is that it doesn't firm up!

Another variable option is using a chocolate bar, perhaps warming it slightly in a microwave to soften it before using it. Using strawberries or other fruit of your choice is also a wonderful approach. Many people I have spoken with expressed a desire to use whipped cream out of a spray can as an excellent approach.

Blindfold Massage

Blindfold

Lotion of your choice

Soothing music

Clean towels

This recipe should rub everyone the right way! Whenever we are deprived of any one sense our other five senses become magnified much stronger than usual. With this little recipe for love your sense of touch and smell will become enhanced, possibly even your sense of taste depending on your personal preferences!

To begin you will need a willing partner stripped down to the buff and a nice smelling (or tasting) lotion. It will help make things more interesting if you remember to also take your clothes off! Before your partner lies down, she needs to securely tie your blindfold in place.

Now the fun begins, as your lover starts by laying on her stomach for the massage. Go slowly now, focus on the feel of your fingertips, and notice what part of her body you are applying the lotion to. Does the fragrance seem different? Is it stronger, or do you also notice other smells? Continue slowly on her back, and then ask her to roll over on her back, but only when she is ready. When she is on her back pay special attention to her reaction to your touch. In those frontal areas that she reacts to are the places to linger just a little longer. Nature will soon take its course, but for the added affect leave your blindfold on until you are spent.

Afterplay, Keep the Love Light Burning

Popcorn

Paper

Scented lotion

Grapes

Strawberries

Chocolate

There seems to be so much written about foreplay and the many methods of lovemaking, but virtually nothing about what could possibly happen after the lovemaking has finished. It appears the generally understood thought is that the man usually falls asleep in about two minutes or less! Come on now guys, we can make a better showing than that if we have a plan. Over the years I have heard many a woman complain that once a guy is done and rolls over he is out for the rest of the night! Kaput, finished, wasted, and out of the loop. Men, we can change that habit if we set our mind to do it(To not fall asleep that is).

With a little forethought before we make love we could preset our minds to do other things than fall asleep. Some of the things to consider doing after making love might be popcorn shooters. This means you would need to pop the corn well in advance or buy a bag already popped. Popcorn shooting means that you roll up a sheet of paper into a funnel and while lying on your back drop a kernel of popcorn into the funnel and blow it straight up in the air for your lover to catch with her mouth, no hands! Let it be a contest and take turns with your lover. Also doing the same thing with grapes is a nice alternative to popcorn. I personally prefer strawberries dipped in chocolate as a wonderful sensual interlude. If your energy level allows, you could ask your partner to lie on her side and you lie beside her and give her a slow massage with a nice lotion. This could be a nice way to top off your lovemaking, or rekindle the fires of passion!

PANTIES BY THE YEAR

Assortment of panties purchased over time

Nice "I Love You" card

This is another scenario that leaves you many options to exercise. This idea is that you will simply give your lover a pair of panties on a recurring basis. This might be once a month, once a week, or whenever you choose over the period of a year.

You need to start by buying her a nice card and then write in the card, or use the attached certificate, that notes she will receive a new pair of panties every month, week, etc. At one time I saw an ad in Playboy magazine where you could subscribe to a service that would send your lover a new pair of sexy panties every month,

---

GIFT CERTIFICATE

TO:_____, this certificate hereby entitles you to receive from me a new pair of panties every_____.

Signed: _____Date: _____

Do not be alarmed if you are asked to model the panties upon receipt of each new pair!

THE TWELVE DAYS OF LOVE

Twelve items/notes/flowers/jewelry

This recipe follows the same general concept as the twelve days of Christmas song. Instead of leading up to Christmas, the 12 days lead up to a special day for you and your lover. It may be an event as simple as her birthday, a holiday, and anniversary or just for the romance of it all in your wonderful life!

This can be fun without being very expensive to do. Day one through day twelve you give your love a small gift leading up to the grand finale on the twelfth day. Examples of these gifts might be a small bottle of perfume; flowers, a love note, balloons, jewelry, clothing or most any nice thing will work!

It would also be a nice touch if you could think of a theme to hook into, such as hearts, flowers, etc. If by chance your love collects any specific thing you could use to focus on, i.e.: cows, ducks, pigs, teddy bears or chickens. This could easily form a common thread for the entire twelve days.

THE TRAIL OF LOVE

24 roses

1 bottle of wine

2 wine glasses

1 teddy or equivalent

2 or more printed signs

Soothing music

This is sure to put some spark into that adventurous woman in your life. A little mystery and adventure is good for anyone's libido! The plot of this is for you to arrange a trail of roses and notes that leads your lady to discover you in the buff (or just about nude) waiting to fulfill her most erotic fantasies.

Simply set the scene when she is not there with you, but you know what time she is due to return. Start with putting a sign on the door that instructs her to follow the trail of roses that will guide her to you, picking up the roses as she goes.

I offer this example to better illustrate the "Trail of Love". On the front door is a note with instructions. As she steps inside the door there is a trail of roses for her to follow. The flower trail leads her to the master bedroom where she finds a note instructing her to put on whatever sexy little thing that is laid out on the bed for her, perhaps a teddy, panties, etc. After she changes she picks up on the rose trail again, now the trail takes her into the kitchen where there is a note telling her to remove the bottle of bubbly and continue to follow the rose trail. The trail now leads her to where you are with 2 wine glasses and an empty flower vase for the roses. From there you simply follow nature's course.

THE TASTE OF LOVE

Blindfold

Grapes

Chocolate

Candy bits

Beverages

Tasty morsels

This is probably the simplest of recipes yet! You just start out by blind-folding your partner and informing that person that you will be feeding them various wonderful things and that they are to guess what these things are. Make sure that you have adequate privacy and have set some ambience for this fine endeavor.

A little mood music in the background would also be a nice touch! It is best to plan ahead and arrange to have a supply of goodies to sample. As with all games that lovers play, take your time and take your turn. This will bring your love to a slow simmer…

Any little variation you can add to this would be welcomed by your partner. Don't be afraid to experiment, just start out gently.

THE EROTICA OF SILENCE

Music

Candles (Optional)

We have all heard that saying, "Silence is golden". With this recipe silence does turn your loving into solid gold! Typically during foreplay and love-making most people verbalize their feelings and wants.

With this approach tell your lover that neither of you can speak for the duration of your lovemaking. This is much like both of you being mutes. You become forced to communicate non-verbally, by touch and gesture only. If you start to feel frustrated just relax and take a few deep breaths and then you will be ready to go again. Take your time and guide your partner's head and hands and move them gently to get your needs met. Remember that both of you need to participate in this type of lovemaking or probably only one person will have a happy outcome.

To add a different wrinkle to this try putting a blindfold on both of you. This way your sensory system is reduced to only smell and taste, no sight, no sound and only the tactile touch of your body. Your sense of touch and physical feelings should be greatly enhanced by closing off two sensory systems. This sensory experience can be highly erotic for both partners.

THE ARTISTRY OF LOVE

1 Set of Body Paints

Music

The artistry of love conjures up many wonderful possibilities in the mind. Just the act of making love in a beautiful and sensuous way is also truly artistry in motion. Touching the human body in a certain way guarantees a set of responses, much like a violinist playing his instrument and eliciting the beauty of music. Try to think of the artist who with each stroke of his brush creates beauty, simple or complex. Whatever your taste in art might be, impressionism to abstract, there is much beauty to create and behold.

With your body paints in hand, ask your lover to disrobe and lay down where she might be comfortable. I would recommend painting only one body side per session, or let that be dictated by your self-control. Starting with the body side of her choice let the creative juices flow through your fingertips into the brush in your hand. Be sure to take your time and pay attention to all the fine details; be sure to wisely incorporate her body features into your art. Also use all of her body's gentle swells and slopes, using colors that compliment her skin tone.

ROSE PETALS

2 roses (Your choice of color)

1 rose scented candle

Romantic music

The essence of this loving situation is to start with two or more roses. First fold the bed down with the bottom sheet exposed. Now take one rose and remove all the petals and spread them over the bed. Secondly, take the next rose and carefully remove all the thorns from the stem. Place the thorn less rose on the center of her pillow. Feel free to do anything to enhance the ambiance of the bedroom, including soft lights, music, and soft sheets. A rose scented candle/incense will put the finishing touches on the scene. Now the seductions begins!

Assuming that you have now persuaded your lover to join you in the bedroom, by all means be prepared to take your time. Help her undress and indulge yourself in many long loving caresses with your fingers, and certainly do not forget to exercise your tongue! After you gently assist your lover in laying down, scoop up the rose petals and sprinkle them over her body. Take time to cover each nipple and her belly button with a rose petal. Very slowly take the thornless rose and use it on her body like a paint brush, much like an artist painting a masterpiece. Use very gentle strokes that start at her lips and slowly work your way down. Also make sure when you get to her breasts that you take the rose and cover one nipple at a time and then holding the rose stem between the palms of both hands slowly make the rose swirl over her nipple ever so lightly. After giving each nipple this treat, continue to "paint" your way down her body with special attention to her inner thighs. Take your time and be creative, and above all, enjoy!

POETRY, THE LANGUAGE OF LOVE

Poetry

One rose

Candles

Wine (or other beverage)

Poetry come in different styles, but none more splendid than the poetry of love. There have been countless volumes wrote on the subject of love. This recipe of love requires you to find two or more books of poetry that focuses on the subject of love. Browning is one of my favorites, but there is a huge amount available.

Now make a date with your lover, a time when the kids are in bed and the pets are in their kennels. Find a comfortable place for the two of you to sit and face one another. Pour the glasses of wine (or your beverage of choice). Now is the time to give her the rose. Using whatever you have, a fireplace, candles or incense, fire them up to complete the ambiance!

Settle back now and slowly read your love a poem out loud. When that is completed it is time for both of you to talk about the poem. How did it make you feel? Can you relate to anything in the poem? Continue on with the next poem only when she says she is ready to move on. Now it is her turn to read the poem.

Enjoy the moments and words; savor the romance and feelings as they flood in. Let the mood take you both where it may!

WEDDING VOWS, ONCE IS NEVER ENOUGH

Anniversary ring

Copy of your wedding vows

Flowers

Romantic Atmosphere

Would you do your wedding all over again? This could be the opportunity to renew your vows, just like staging your wedding all over again!

For some people, re-staging the whole wedding all over again is totally out of the question! Can you remember the heartburn and agonizing over all the details of your wedding? That though alone could trigger nightmares for some couples.

What maybe an easier and saner idea would be to surprise your love by staging an unrehearsed reading of your wedding vows for just the two of you. You will need to find a quiet and hopefully a romantic place that you can read your vows to her. You can read all the vows, or make two sets of your wedding vows and highlight the words she can read. If it were appropriate and affordable at the time, it would be especially nice to coincide this event with your wedding anniversary and present her with an anniversary ring!

There could be numerous variations you could do with this theme. Let your sense of romance and adventure take over and enjoy wherever love may take you and your loved one!

LOVE NOTES

Assorted Post-It Notes

Assorted colored ink pens

Ribbons/bows

This is an amazingly simple but meaningful thing for you to do for your loved one. Start with writing some romantic notes on different Post-It Notes to place all over the house. The notes could vary from a simply "I love you" to "You hold my heart in your hands", or "Take me, I'm your love monkey".

To add a little more flair to this concept you could use ink pens with many different colors of ink, or add a bow or a simple string ribbon with each note.

What will be the result? There are endless possibilities here. It may be a good idea to check earlier in the day to see what kind of day your lover is having before putting this plan in motion. No one having a terribly bad day really wants to walk into a romantic situation and feel expected to shift gears immediately.

There are countless messages that you could come up with. Many couples develop their own little terms of endearments, these would be some that would be highly desirable to use. Let your little love light shine!

CAMPERS ALERT

Tent

One large sleeping bag

Flashlight

This will certainly test the sense of adventure in both of you! What adds a different wrinkle to this concept is that you don't leave home to go camping.

You can do this right in your own back yard! Of course I wasn't referring to this as a wintertime activity, unless you feel the strong sense of adventure to do so.

First I would suggest using a tent for maximum privacy in this adventure. If privacy is a huge issue for you and your lover, you could camp out right on the living room floor. Just turn out all the lights and make believe you are in the wilderness.

If you are outside as originally intended, this would be the wonderful opportunity for both of you to lay on your backs and enjoy the star lit evening. This should easily provide the opportunity for some intimate and romantic conversation. Take your time and start with just enjoying being together and talking as only lovers can do. The rest of the evening will take care of itself.

Remember to leave your cell phone and beeper in the house because the evening belongs to star struck lovers, not friends or family bugging you.

THE MYSTERY DATE

Excellent Restaurant

Nightclub for Dancing

Floral Shop

Dinner theater

Horse drawn carriage

To accomplish a mystery date will take a great deal of time and advanced planning. There is also a great deal of variables that you can incorporate depending where you live and the resources available to you. The general scope of this concept is for you to plan three or more activities for you and your lover to do together.

Start by telling her you want to make a date with her, usually on a Saturday or Sunday if you both work. Inform her that this is a mystery date and you can tell her no more. Typically you might start with making reservations at an extremely nice restaurant, and then plan two or more things to do for the evening.

To further illustrate this I offer the following example; Dinner reservations for two at the most chic restaurant in town. After dinner a stroll down the street to the flower shop where you have previously arranged to have a bouquet of roses waiting. From there it is just another short stroll to the place where you enter a white horse drawn carriage for a ride around the park.

As stated earlier, there is no end to the variables you can include. You can bet that your lover will be most receptive and appreciative.

OUR SPECIAL POEM

Notebook

2 Ink pens

Mood music

Poetry is something beautiful for the heart and soul. The twist to this approach is that you and your lover will jointly write a poem!

It's not a difficult as it sounds. The hardest part is probably going to be trying to sweep away all the daily concerns and frustrations so you both can focus on this task of love. Take your time to clear away those concerns of the day. You may even want to turn off the phone and beeper.

As you begin you will need to alternate paragraphs. Be patient and thoughtful of each other. Some people can write more easily than others. Try to set a goal of six or more verses the first time. If this works well for both of you, then you may want to attempt a much longer poem with the number of verses divisible by two so you both can be equally involved.

A good warm-up exercise is to read three or four poems out loud to one another to set the mood and firmly readjust the mindset from the pressures of the day. Some people make beautiful music; you both can make beautiful poetry. If you both really like the poetry you have created I would recommend you have it framed and display it proudly.

ALPHABETICAL LOVE

26 flowers/candy

26 notes

Scotch tape

Assorted colors of ink

Flower vase

This simple little ditty will take you all the way back to the first grade! This will also test your memory of the alphabet as it did mine. With only twenty-six letters in the alphabet you will need twenty-six (26) flowers or twenty-six pieces of your choice of candy.

The real challenging part here is to write on all twenty-six cards. I would recommend that first you go through and print in red ink a letter of the alphabet on each card. Then go through and write a love note on each card using that letter of the alphabet. A good example might be; A is for the angel you are in my life, or B is for the beauty with which you decorate my life. Then print those words angel and beauty in red ink so they really will stand out!

It does pose a little challenge to do that with all twenty six letters, but if you will sweep away all the concerns of the day and focus on your loved one you will be pleasantly surprised how easily the thoughts will come pouring out on the paper!

Once you have completed all the cards, then get out the tape and attach the notes one at a time to the flower stems or pieces of candy. Don't forget a nice vase to put the flowers in, or a basket for the candy. Your option here is to decide if you will have the flowers/candy delivered, or deliver them yourself!

LOVE STORY

2 Ink pens

Wire bound notebook

Background music

Allotted "together" time

This could be the opportunity for both of you to write that love story. Really, any story line will work. Whatever the two of you prefer: Romance, mystery or adventure.

To start this project you will need to set the scene with some quiet time around the house so that the two of you are not distracted while you write. Most any type of bound blank paper will work. Its important to keep the story together in one place as it may take more that one session to complete. Simply take turns writing a paragraph at a time.

The person that writes the first paragraph will be setting the tone for the story to follow. I would recommend starting the first paragraph with either something very romantic or very sexy. This could very well influence how the remainder of the evening goes for the two of you.

CALENDAR FULL OF LOVE

24"x30" calendar

Time set aside for both of you

Mood music

This is a simple little ditty to do! It requires that you find a large calendar. Those large desktop types would work very well for this endeavor.

With your partner, start filling in all the usual birthdays and events that are normally celebrated by both of you. Once those are out of the way then talk with your love about remembering those "first" sort of things you shared. Perhaps your first date, first kiss, and all those other wonderful first type of events and then add those to the calendar (Or guess at the dates) . Just reminiscing about those romantic "firsts" can set a whole different tone to the evening, a most loving and romantic tone I hope!

Then with those other days of the year that you have not added anything to, just simply go through and taking turns adding various loving and inspirational thoughts to fill up those vacant days on the calendar.

Upon your completion you will both have a very "special" calendar that speaks of your love every day.

A Flair for Dining Out

Restaurant with ambience

Musician

Flowers

Small, meaningful gift

It has been often said that all the world loves a lover and I have found that to be very true. Nothing starts an evening out better than going to a restaurant that has intimate charm and a romantic atmosphere. This is NOT an evening to dine out at the local burger joint. It will require some real effort to find a wonderful place to eat that has some romantic charm about it. Don't hesitate to ask other people for names of restaurants.

Once you find that special place to dine, make reservations for a Friday or Saturday evening. Also don't be shy about dressing up! Then call a florist and arrange to have a bouquet of flowers delivered to the restaurant. If at all possible try to hire a musician to arrive shortly after you to play at least three songs. Try to make at least one song a favorite of hers. Then also before hand purchase a small but meaningful gift to present to her before the main course.

Then, depending on how the evening goes you may want to go out dancing or return home to fulfill this evening of love.

HOT TUBBING, HOT LOVING

Hot tub

Romantic music

Cold drinks

Maximum privacy

Scented candles

Amorous attitude

Spending time in whirling warm water of a hot tub can be both a relaxing and inspiring time! I believe the true magic here is in the attitude of both people involved in this lighthearted activity. If you do not have a hot tub of your own to use, they can usually be rented by the hour or half hour in your general area. These public rentals are usually clean and will afford you maximum privacy. In your own home you have the ability to arrange for as much privacy as needed.

To help set the stage for this endeavor I would recommend starting with some music that both of you find romantic and enjoyable. Be careful to not let the level of the music become too loud and become a distraction, unless you want the music to cover-up other sounds! Scented candles always add a nice touch to this atmosphere. Be sure it's not a scent that your loved one is allergic to. The music playing and the scented candles working their charm combined with your amorous mood could lead to many wonderful and amazing things happening in that hot tub. Remember to go slowly so no one gets hurt in that slippery situation!

SKINNY DIPPING

Body of Water

Towels

A warm summer evening

Strong sense of adventure

This recipe will charge your batteries! The subject of skinny-dipping going back a long way, probably to the beginning of history. The most alluring aspect of this scenario is the thrill of the risk of getting caught! A sense of risk always seems to get the blood pumping and fires up one's imagination to figure out how to get away with it without getting caught in the raw by other people.

There are a number of possibilities of places you could use; of course a private swimming pool would be the most ideal situation to have. This way you would have maximum privacy and time would not be a cause to feel hurried. If you and your honey bunny let yourselves feel rushed then the romantic adventure becomes less fun.

You could also consider using other places, especially after dark! This would help you minimize the chance of getting seen by others. Such places as a lake, pond or a river could offer you some interesting potential. Sometimes we have to work within our given situation with what is available. The opportunity to frolic about with your loved one in the water after dark could offer you both some intriguing opportunities! Let your sense of adventure take you away and reawaken your youthful sense of adventure that you once had.

KISS TREE

Assorted, foil wrapped chocolate kisses

Wire tree (craft store)

Hot glue gun/tape

Weighted vase

This may cause a few of you out there to have to stretch yourself to get this recipe working for you. For the romantically challenged the concept of a wire tree makes no sense at all. Ok guys; now think back to those weddings where they had a "money tree" on the table. This metal tree can be normally found in most any craft store in white or green. The color is your choice, but I would recommend using the white wire tree. Before you leave that craft store make sure you ask one of those crafty people that work there for some help in finding a "weighted" vase that will support this metal tree.

Once you have gathered all the recommended ingredients you can start by putting the wire tree into the vase and spread out the metal branches so they are nicely separated. Now comes the tricky part. If you are one of those people who are all thumbs you're in big trouble at this point! There are a couple of different ways to attach those foil wrapped chocolate kisses to the metal branches of the tree. You could use a glue gun. If you do, I urge you to experiment with it before working on the real thing. Another option here is that you could use clear scotch tape to delicately tape the foil kisses to the metal branches. Oh no, I know what your thinking, but you must leave the foil on the chocolate kisses! Maybe you could trade a kiss for a kiss. There are many interesting possibilities!

COUPON TREE

Coupons, 12 or more

Glue gun

Metal craft tree

Weighted vase

This is a new twist to the romantic coupon books that have been around for a long time. Instead of giving your special someone a coupon book you will be giving her a tree with these great love coupons. You can buy a book of those love coupons and use the pre-printed coupons, or be adventurous and write your own! If you write your own you might want to start with a visit to a stationary store and buy some attractive paper notes. These typically come blank with a nice border printed on them in a 3"x5" size.

On each card you may want to print what she can redeem that particular card for with you. An example might be, "Redeem this card with Randy for a long and loving kiss". Just set your mind free and you can come up with a whole array of wonderful coupons. For those readers who are experiencing a creative block I offer the following suggestions for topics for the coupons.

Backrubs
Foot massages
Read poetry/short story
Full body massages
Shampoo her hair
Kiss

Back wash in the tub
Doing the supper dishes
Washing her car
Dinner out at her favorite place
Visit to a spa/hot tub
Tickets for the theater

LANGUAGE OF LOVE

Note cards

Flowers

Scotch tape

It has been said that the language of love is only truly spoken in the heart as mere words cannot due justice to love. In this case we will come fairly close as we exercise the language of love on an international basis. There are as many ways to say "I love you" as there is languages in the world. This concept maybe one of the most challenging in this book.

To make this work you need to find how to say "I love you" in as many languages as possible! Yes, this is truly a challenge, but by using the public library or a personal computer you will be surprised by how easily this will start to come together for you.

Once your research has been completed, then you are ready to move onto the next step. Fill in each card with the foreign language saying I love you. An example would be : "I love you, Randy" or "Ich liebe dich, Randy".

Then scotch tape each card to a flower to form a special bouquet of love for her! Despite how difficult this seems, it is well worth doing for the love you will receive in return.

FISH BOWL

Clear fish bowl

24 stationary notes

Multi-color ink pens

OK guys, now I know that this is one recipe where you will no doubt excel with the greatest of ease. It has been said that romancing is just a prelude to sexual fulfillment. Most of us guys will normally make some attempt at romance with the great hope that it will culminate in sexual activity!

From a stationary store find some attractive looking note cards with hearts or some pleasant border on them. Now here comes the easy part for your creativity. On each card write down something erotic and sexual to do!

I told you this would be easy! These could be something as simple as a body massage with oils, a bath together. Your imagination can take over from there!

The fish bowl can be found at a pet store or hobby store, or even a nice little wicker basket would be a nice touch. Put all the cards in the bowl and give them to your love. Tell her she can use this anytime she wants by drawing only one card out at a time, but she cannot peek when drawing the card out!

The only real limitation to this recipe is your imagination and sexual motivation.

Mountain of Candy

Styrofoam ball, 12″

Shallow bowl

"T" straight pins

Mini candy bars

Plastic wrap

Red or pink ribbon, 24″

Candy is dandy and wonderful for putting love in the air. By now you probably know what kind of candy bars your loved one likes the very best. There used to be a bit a of saying years ago that candy is dandy, but liquor is quicker! We will have to save that idea for another recipe at another time.

Most of the ingredients for this recipe can be easily found at most any craft store.

First put the Styrofoam ball it in a bowl or on some sort of a pedestal so it will not roll around while you are working on it. Starting on the bottom of the ball and going around it in a circular fashion attach the mini candy bars with the "T" straight pins. After the first row is put on the ball, start the second and successive rows by going up half the length of the candy bar. You could also alternate rows of mini candy bar types if you prefer as you work your way to the top.

Once you have the mini candy bars in place, then set the entire arrangement on a sheet of plastic wrap and pull the sides up to the top. Then wrap it all up with a ribbon and tie it into a bow on top.

STUFFED LOVE

Stuffed animal

Jewelry

Plastic wrap

Long red ribbon and bow

Dinner reservations

I have never over the years found a woman who did not like jewelry and stuffed animals so it seems only fitting that we combine both elements to make for yet another wonder recipe of love and romance. Since jewelry is the order of the day it is also highly recommended that you consider this recipe for such occasions as anniversaries and birthdays, or better yet, just as another way to tell her how much you love her.

First identify her favorite animal or stuffed animal. Do not include your old animal self in this selection! Maybe there is a stuffed animal she already has that you can use, or don't be a tight wad, just buy a new one. The jewelry must be chosen carefully to compliment your loved one. One piece of jewelry on the stuffed animal is nice, but also consider accessorizing the stuffed animal with earrings, necklace, bracelet and ring.

Once the stuffed animal has the jewelry on it, wrap it in plastic and add the ribbon and bow. Take it to the restaurant where you have made reservations a few hours prior to arriving. Instruct the wait staff to bring the stuffed animal to your table when you ask for dessert. The rewards for your effort will be tenfold.

CREAMY LOVING

Chocolate whipped cream

Strawberry whipped cream

Vanilla whipped cream

Hope you have an appetite for this one! It promises to arouse your sense of taste to new levels! It all starts with that trip to the grocery store to get the supplies that you will need for this evening or afternoon of pure sensual delight.

At the grocery store start by looking for the aerosol cans of whipped cream. This works so much better than the plastic tubs of whipped cream. At the larger stores I have had no trouble finding a selection of flavors of whipped creams in a can. If variety is not a concern, go ahead and stop at the corner quick mart store. Try to keep in mind her preference as well as your taste preference!

When the opportunity and mood presents itself, let the games begin! Ask your lover to assume a comfortable position on the bed in the buff. Then take your time and strategically squirt out the whipped cream in all the areas that you believe to be the most sensual. It's always nice to ask your lover for a little guidance as you administer the whipped cream. I shouldn't need to say this, but I must. Now slowly and carefully lick all the whipped cream off your lover. If the situation allows, ask your lover to do the same for you.

Flavors are optional!

Sweet Loving

12+assorted candy bars

12+small strips of paper

Small basket or bowl

Colored plastic wrap

This recipe is in the category of nearly being a no brainer! Sometimes we can tend to overlook the more obvious things in life. You can start this adventure by making a trip to the supermarket or your local hobby store. Yes, even hobby stores have candy bars, I believe you will find a better selection of candy bars at the supermarket. You can opt to buy a large assortment of candy bars, or if your lover has only one favorite type of candy bar, you may want to purchase that brand only!

On the 12+strips of paper write down different things you would like to do for your lover. Your choice, and since you are the one who will be performing whatever you put on the paper, make sure it is something you would like to do! It could be something as simple as going out to the movies or to dinner at her favorite restaurant, or some wonderful and beautiful things to be done in the bedroom! I would really recommend that you cover a wide range of possibilities in your offerings.

Place these candy bars with the strips of paper taped to the backside of all the candy bars and use the colored plastic wrap as a filler in the basket to help the candy bars stand erect! Explain to your lover that only one coupon a day can be redeemed.

ROSE PANTIES

Rose formed panties, 6+

Mood music

Refreshments

This is quite a simple little ditty to undertake. There is really such a thing as rose-formed panties. This is where the panty is folded in such a way it looks like a rose bud attached to a green metal stem. The real challenge here is to find a store that sells these! The first place that comes to my mind is Spencer's Gifts, a store you would usually find in most malls. If they do not have it in stock ask them to order them in for you. What would add that additional flair would be to add six chocolate roses to round out the bouquet.

A good part of the fun is trying to persuade her to model them for you! This opens up a whole host of interesting possibilities for the two of you.

Let your mind and imagination run amuck with all the sensual possibilities that could be generated. The only true boundaries for a real romantic is your imagination. Enjoy!

Nostalgic Romance

Auto

AM/FM, Cassette or CD Player

Selection of music from your high school years, or Barry White or Elvis Presley music

This is a trip into the past, probably right around your high school years I would guess. Your vehicle or the one you had access to was probably where a good amount of your romantic endeavors took place. Many, many years ago they used to call it "spooning" or romancing, where a couple would sit together for hours talking and kissing, and anything else she would let you get away with!

To put together an evening like this you just need to load up your loved one in the car in the evening and away you go. In preparation, some easy listening or easy loving music is in order. It would help you if you knew what type of romantic music or singer she preferred. A little soda to sip on in between the kissing and hugging would be a nice touch!

Ideally, it would be nice to go and park where you can see the moon in all its splendor. Parking somewhere overlooking a lake with moonlight shining across the water is a great touch. If no body of water is available then I would suggest finding a place to park on high ground with some very distant lights to look at.

Take your time with her, don't be in a rush. Maybe make the entire evening a date just like those high school years. Just let the magic happen!

A Mid-Summer's Afternoon

Picnic basket full of goodies to eat

Old blanket

Bottle of wine

Quiet picnic area

Ok fellows, I probably should not need to say a thing about how to put this all together! The main way to botch this up would be for you to bring along a radio and listen to a sports show or talk radio. That is a large part of the reason why I chose to leave the radio or tape player off the list in this recipe. Enjoy the sounds of silence and the conversation that your lover has to share with you, and above all remember to listen!

To make this extra special for your lover, prepare the picnic basket with some nice food. There is a wide variety to choose from: Cheeses, meats, and breads. Always try to keep her preferences in food in mind when shopping to fill the picnic basket. Probably a quick trip by the deli at your local supermarket will provide everything you need to fill that basket to the brim with goodies! Don't forget to put an old blanket in the car so you can have something to sit on while enjoying the food.

Try to make this adventure a date with your lover. Don't rush anything, just savor each moment as it develops and the rewards will come to you in many wonderful ways!

A Candlelight Dinner for Two

Cornish hens (2)

Stovetop dressing

Cranberry sauce

1 can of sweet corn

Sweet pickles

Green & black olives

White wine

I know that a few of you are reading this and thinking that a candlelight dinner is pretty lame, but it does the romantic trick! Those of you that are more advanced cooks in the kitchen may certainly want to alter the items on the list for dinner. For guys like myself who suffer from being among the culinary challenged, this simple but nice dinner is quite elegant and nearly foolproof.

At the supermarket you may want to go ahead an get a prepared relish tray to help keep it simple. The Cornish hens are easy once they are thawed out. Usually the cooking instructions are right on the wrapper. Slide the hens in the oven and baste with a little butter spray. Just follow the instructions on the Stove Top dressing package. I prefer the microwave packages because they are easier and faster. Go ahead and heat up the corn with a pat of butter for flavoring. Ensure that the cranberry sauce has been chilled in the fridge and if you have the canned sauce make sure you slice it.

For the table setting go all out with napkins, plates, silverware, wine glasses and candleholders. Wait and light the candles when you are ready to sit down and eat.

After you pour the wine make sure you offer a toast to your loved one before beginning the meal. Bon Appetite!

A Summer's Evening

A warm evening

Porch swing

Iced drinks

This probably sounds way to simple to be any good. Trust me on this one; it set the scene for bigger and better things!

It would be good to check her frame of mind before embarking on an adventure like this. If she is still hacked off at you for peeing on the toilet seat, then this would not be a good time!

Check the fridge to see what you have to drink that's cold, maybe enough wine for two, or soda? Be sure you prepare in your stealth mode before beginning.

Invite your lover to join you outside for a little time on the swing and some conversation. Don't hog the conversation; make sure you ask her how she is doing and feeling. Only listen to her talk about what's on her mind and do not offer any solutions unless she ask you for help! Women usually want someone to listen but not fix their problems. Beware; you could be one of her problems!

If possible just sit there and hold her hand and gently swing. That can be very soothing all by itself. Just allow the evening to go where it may! If you are not in a hurry the whole evening will go off real well!

ROW, ROW YOUR BOAT

Row boat (Rental?)

Picnic basket

Parasol (umbrella)

Beverages

This is kind of a nostalgic throw back to fifty years ago. This way you will have her undivided attention providing everyone turns off their cell phones and beepers! Technology is great, but at times a real pain in the neck when you are in the mood for romance.

The place to start with this quest would be to find a lakeside boat rental business. You will need to check this out beforehand so you don't get any bad surprises. Reserve the rowboat if you can. Other types of boats just won't do for this scenario.

Also before hand, arrange to have your picnic basket and beverages ready to roll. The parasol is a nice romantic touch that is seen in many old romantic movies. While you row, your lover opens the parasol and uses it to shade herself from the sun.

I would recommend you start rowing out to the middle of the lake, and once you get there and catch your breath, lunch is served! Just let the boat float about and spend that quality time with your lover engaged in quality conversation. I would not suggest going much further with this adventure unless you both swim! In this day and age of equal opportunity you could probably row her out and she would insist on rowing the boat back to the shore!

A Walk on the Wild Side

Decent walking shoes

Dress lightly

Lunch money

Zoo/park

Most ladies will tell you that a slow walk through the park holding hands can be very romantic in nature. Dressing appropriately for the occasion is an important place to start. Athletic shoes of some sort would probably be the shoes of choice. The main thing here is that you don't have sore or blistered feet!

You will want to make a date of it; go ahead and ask her out! Kind of makes you feel like a teenager all over again. This will also help set a positive sense of expectancy for the event. Listen up now guys; it is important that throughout this walk that you stroll at her pace and remember to hold her hand in yours as you go out and about. My recommendations would that you start with your local zoo or a nice park, even a museum will work. Tend to key in on her likes and dislikes so it will be the most pleasurable experience for both of you.

After that slow stroll out and about, then the time is right to stop in for a light lunch or brunch at a quiet laid back sort of place. At the very least stop by a coffee house. When you return home I would suggest both of you head for the shower at the same time. What a great way to cap off a delightful afternoon but with an afternoon delight!

Romantic Food Section

Romantic food, yes there really is such a thing. Any of the great romantic stories over the ages speaks of food and drink as a kind of magical elixir for lovers. Currently you can find numerous books on the market that speak also of food and romance. The one book that leaps to my mind is the book titled, "Stories for the Chocolate Lover's Soul".

Chocolate seems to do wonderful things when women eat it! It truly does something special with their brain chemistry. I slept through most of my science classes so I am basically clueless to the scientific explanation of how it works! The main thing is that I know it greatly affects the mood of women, and I have witnessed that first hand! The only way I can come close to explaining it is that chocolate seems to act like a mild aphrodisiac in virtually all women I have ever known, and believe me when I say it's been a lot of women I've known!

The recipes in this book are all highly workable and seem tasty to me. I have tried to keep the recipes short and fairly simple to do. My thought is that the more user friendly the recipes are, the more likely that you guys will give them a try! After all I am asking you to enter the inner sanctum of the kitchen world! There really is no big mystery about how to get around in the kitchen. I believe the real trick for guys to learn is to exercise their patience. Following these recipes is every bit as simple as following the instructions in a repair manual to fix something mechanical. Can you remember back to all those times when you followed the instructions to assemble something or to repair that car yourself? Sure you do, now think how very proud you were of your accomplishment. The proven track record is already there, and now it is the time to take your abilities to a new level. There is a Buddhist saying that really seems to fit here: "The journey of a thousand miles begins with the first step". It is time to step up now to the kitchen.

You can do it guys! I have faith in you, and after your first time fixing one of these recipes in the kitchen you will also gain a whole new feeling of competence in the kitchen! Like the saying goes, "the proof is in the pudding", or something to that effect!

LOVING IN MARGRITAVILLE

1½ cup of finely crushed pretzel crumbs

½ cup of sugar

½ cup melted margarine

14 ounces sweetened condensed milk

1 cup chopped fresh strawberries

¾ cup limejuice

4 tablespoons of tequila

2 tablespoons of triple sec

4 drops of red food coloring

1 cup of whipped cream

Loving her in margaritaville, what a wonderful thought! This little recipe is outstanding in the summer when you want something to beat the heat. Candy is dandy, but liquor is quicker!

For this gourmet treat we start by lightly buttering a 9-inch pie plate. Now mix up the pretzel crumbs, sugar and margarine, then press firmly into the pie plate bottom and sides to make the crust. In a large bowl mix the sweetened milk, chopped strawberries, lime, tequila, triple sec and food coloring. Now mix in the whipped cream slowly. Pour it all into the piecrust and freeze about 4 hours or until stiff. You guys do know how to recognize something stiff! Believe me, there are so many sensual ways to enjoy this!

QUICKIE HAWAIIAN PORK

2 pounds of pork

1 can of pineapple chunks

¼ cup of white vinegar

1 teaspoon of ginger

Instant rice, prepared

I believe that everyone probably enjoys a quickie now and then, and this quickie will be no exception! It is a fun little dish to do for lunch or the supper meal. There is nothing wrong with cooking up a special meal to share with your honey bunny. No doubt she will greatly appreciate all your effort. This little dish could be the centerpiece of the meal.

First we need to cut the pork into 1-inch cubes. Then in a large cooking type skillet place all the ingredients and start cooking. Plan on simmering for about an hour. The longer you cook the more tender the pork will be. When you are ready to serve it up, just pour it over rice and you will have a spectacular dish!

Relax and enjoy the meal with your honey and have nice tropical thoughts for both of you! While being in your dining room isn't even close to being in the Hawaiian Islands, you can certainly do everything possible to create that special effect. You may want to consider going to the local craft store and buy some cheap paper decoration to spruce up the scene. Some paper pineapples, paper flowers, and steel guitar music would produce a very special ambiance for you and your lover. Go for it Tiger!

CHOCOLATE CHOO-CHOO EXPRESS

6 tablespoons of chocolate liqueur

1 envelope of plain gelatin

1-½ cups of hot black coffee

2 cups of fat-free chocolate ice cream

This recipe will certainly put you on the road to the chocolate choo choo express will definitely take the edge off of the day for you. It will sneak up on you and let half the air out of your tires. What a great way to unwind! As I have said before, wherever you find chocolate you find the secret ingredient for a loving attitude. That alone is enough inspiration to go to the kitchen and get started.

You can start by putting the liqueur and gelatin in a blender and then add the hot coffee and blend until the gelatin granules are fully dissolved. Now go ahead and add the chocolate ice cream and blend the whole thing until it becomes smooth. Pour this mixture into custard or wine goblets and put it in the fridge to get a good chill on it.

Let us not talk calories here, just settle back with your love and enjoy each wonderful bite!

BOURBON PIE

21 large marshmallows

1 cup of whipping cream, whipped

3 tablespoons of bourbon, whatever brand floats your boat!

1 can of evaporated milk

Chocolate pie shell

Nothing like having a little snort of bourbon along with your dessert, it works for me! It is the perfect dish for a real lover to stir up. This would be a golden opportunity to pour booze into the pie and into the cook at the same time.

In the process of cooking, all the alcohol in this recipe does remain in the pie! With any luck you might get a slight buzz if you eat the whole pie! I would guess that the container the bourbon came in still has a small amount left. You might want to take a little snort in the process of cooking this pie.

In a saucepan pour the can of evaporated milk in and add the marshmallows. Simmer this over a low heat and stirring frequently until all the yummy marshmallows are dissolved. Allow the mixture to cool completely and then gently mix in the whipped cream and bourbon. Pour this in to the chocolate pie shell and stick it in the fridge to chill for 6 hours. Your tummy will thank you for this fabulous pie!

SWINGING WINGS

10 chicken wings

½ cup of melted margarine

1 small box of Parmesan cheese

1 teaspoon of garlic powder

Swinging wings, sounds like a swingers club or something! This does seem like an ideal way to swing your wings, sort of! There are some variations you could choose to add to this recipe if it strikes your fancy. I personally like to add about 2 generous pinches of cayenne pepper to the mixture to kick it up a notch! You must go where your taste buds tell you to go!

Start by setting aside the melted margarine and mix up all the other ingredients in a bowl. Now take the chicken wings and dip them in the margarine and then roll them in the dry mixture you made. Then put them in a casserole bowl and pop them in the oven for about 1 hour at 350 degrees. I find it vaguely interesting that so many different dishes are bake at 350 degrees. I guess it must be close to an ideal baking temperature for food?

These swinging wings are good right from the oven, or they do make for good leftovers for a quick bite. They are most excellent with a variety of sauces to dip them in. My personal favorite for dip is honey mustard barbecue sauce although plain ranch dressing works well. Remember to obey your taste buds!

FRITO BANDITO BALLS

2 pounds of lean ground beef

1 cup of Fritos, crushed

1 egg slightly beaten

1 can of cream of mushroom soup

4 ounces of water

Green Tabasco sauce (optional)

Bandito balls with Fritos, sounds pretty wild to me! I think we can make this recipe come alive and sing! I have always been a big fan of Fritos and love the taste of jalapeno sauce. This is one of these crazy dishes where you just have to go with your instinct. A little rice would be a good side dish with this.

First we mix the meat, Fritos and egg together very well. Now we roll this into balls, whatever size you want your balls and then brown them in the skillet. Turn your skillet down to a low heat and pour the soup and water in and simmer for at least thirty minutes. Season with the green Tabasco sauce to suit your taste.

Don't you just love these simple dishes? You could serve these Frito bandito balls with rice or a variety of other Mexican food. Just let your imagination run with this recipe and you will be amply rewarded for your effort. Enjoy the tasty balls of a Frito bandito!

CHOCOLATE LOVING CUSTARD

9" pastry shell

1-ounce semi-sweet chocolate squares

14 ounces sweetened condensed milk

3 eggs, beat them up!

1-½ cups of hot water

2 teaspoons of vanilla extract

4 oz thawed non-dairy whipped cream

Did anyone say chocolate again? I believe it's the food of choice for lovers. This will probably require another trip to the grocery store, but it will be a short trip. Custard is great, but as a chocolate it is a heavenly delight. To start this taste treat just preheat the oven to 425 degrees. In a heavy saucepan, over low heat, melt the chocolate along with sweetened condensed milk. Remove the pan from the heat and stir in the eggs and mix well. Now add hot water and vanilla and mix. Pour it all into the pastry shell and bake for ten minutes. Reduce the oven temperature to 300 degrees and continue baking another 25 minutes or until you can put a knife into the center and it comes out clean! Let it cool and slip it into the fridge. Smear the whipped cream on top and you are ready to eat.

Beware now of this thing called "smearing" whipped cream, this could open up all kinds of possibilities for you!

GRAPES DELIGHT

Green grapes

Red grapes

White chocolate chips

Chocolate chips

Ok guys, this is an actual cooking alert in progress; man the kitchen and fire up the stove! With the grapes, red and green, still in there bunches from the supermarket, wash them gently in the sink and allow them to drain and dry. That's the simple part. Now to melt the chocolate I would recommend that you place one type of the chocolate in a bowl and place the bowl into a pan of water. Put this on a medium heat and when the chocolate is melted (do not bring the chocolate to a boil) we are ready to do it to it! If all else fails, you can always microwave the chocolate chips!

Gently dip the bunch of grapes into the melted chocolate and thoroughly cover the grapes. Now for the tricky part; lift the bunch of grapes out of the pan and hold it over the sink. Gently twirl the bunch of grapes in a back and forth manner to help prevent them from sticking together. Once they have cooled enough to not stick together we are ready to refrigerate them, do not freeze!

After the grapes are well cooled they are ready to eat. You might consider serving them as a bunch, or plucking the grapes from the bunch so they can be handled and eaten separately. How you choose to serve them could be as sensual as serving her each grape between your lips, or by some other erotic mode! Let your imagination take wings and propel you to new heights!

Chocolate Covered Bananas

4 Bananas

4-6″ wooden sticks

1 bag of chocolate chips

Another delightful taste treat to please the senses. One of the interesting things about working with bananas is that they do appear to be a phallic symbol! Hey guys, don't let this freak you out. Look at it as a subtle message for your lover. At the supermarket pick up some ripe bananas. If you are not sure which bananas are ripe just ask some female shopper for advice. I have always found women liberal with their advice. Now march right on over to the isle with the baking goods. It is there you will find those wooden sticks and chocolate. There you must decide if you want dark chocolate or light chocolate. If in doubt, go with the light chocolate as it is usually agreeable with everyone's taste. Look for packages of chocolate chips to use in this recipe.

Now on to the kitchen, men! The thing you need now is usually called a double boiler. If that isn't recognizable then use a large bowl, put the chocolate in it, then place it inside a pan with water. Bring the water to a soft boil and the chocolate should start melting. The easy way out would to be microwave the chocolate. Once it is melted you can peel the banana, shove a stick half way into one end of it and roll the banana in the chocolate, holding it upside down for the extra chocolate to drip off. After refrigerating they are ready to eat. Just take a moment to contemplate the possibilities!

Work on this contemplation thing guys, you don't really want me to draw you a map or anything!

PRETZEL OF LOVE

Round pretzels

Hershey's chocolate kisses

M & M plain candies

Cookie sheet

Salty chocolate is the order of the day! It may sound strange at first, but it's really quite good. After a quick trip to the grocery store you are ready to rock and roll! Remember now, hid your calorie counter under the sink for the next few days.

Lightly coat a cookie sheet with a little spray on oil. Pre-heat your oven to 200 degrees and let the cooking begin. Place the round pretzels on the cookie sheet close enough to touch each other. Now unwrap the chocolate kisses and place one inside each round pretzel. Nothing complicated here! Now place the cookie sheet in the oven for 2 to 3 minutes. Monitor them carefully in the oven; we only want the chocolate kisses to get very soft, not runny. When they appear soft, pull the cookie sheet out of the oven and place it on top the stove. Now for the crowning touch place an M & M candy on top of each chocolate kiss and gently push down to flatten out the kiss. Success is now yours! Place the cookie sheet in the fridge and wait a few minutes until the chocolate kiss firms up again. Then with a spatula place these little jewels on a plate. I recommend chilling them before serving. A salty kiss for your lover is a wonderful thing.

It has been said that chocolate is a great aphrodisiac for lovers, so indulge!

CREAMY CHOCOLATE DELIGHT

1 baked pastry shell

3 semi-sweet chocolate squares

14 ounces of sweetened condensed milk

¼ teaspoon salt

¼ cup hot water

1-teaspoon vanilla extract

1 cup whipped cream

Shaved chocolate

Don't the ladies love something creamy? This is a real yummy little morsel that would get any chocoholic excited! Simply start with a medium heat and melt the chocolate with the sweetened condensed milk and salt in a saucepan. Cook and stir for 5 to 8 minutes until it is very thick and fudgy. Now add water and stir until it thickens and bubbles. Remove the pan from the heat and add vanilla. Let all cool about 15 minutes and then put it in the fridge to chill for about 30 minutes. Now put it all in a large mixing bowl and beat one cup of whipping cream until it gets stiff! Yes, it really does get stiff. Mix it into the chocolate and pour it all into the pastry shell. Refrigerate about three hours, put some whipped cream on top and with a grater shave some chocolate to spread over this wonderful masterpiece.

THE CHOCOLATE MOUSSE IS LOOSE

14 ounces of sweetened condensed milk

1 cup of cold water

1 package of instant chocolate pudding mix

1 cup of whipped cream, whipped

The mousse is loose in the kitchen now! This little recipe is so simple and quick to make, it falls in that category of no brainers. Of course nearly all lovers enjoy the luxury of chocolate. Truly an aphrodisiac of the heart.

Let us begin this short adventure in cooking by mixing all the ingredients except the whipped cream together. Don't be shy about using that electric mixer, go for it. Let everything chill for about ten minutes and then carefully mix the whipped cream into the rest of the ingredients. Now put the mixture into serving glasses. Using wine glasses or champagne glasses gives it a real classy look to it! Also be sure to save enough of the whipped cream so you can put a dab on top of each glass of mousse.

This definitely says "amore" to your lover, and also to yourself. It promises to be a sensual delight from your lips to your tummy! This could be the golden opportunity for you to make this evening a very memorable one for you and your lover! The main thing that could prevent this from happening is you. Tell me it isn't gonna be so?

MACAROON KISSES

7 ounces of flaked coconut

14 ounces of sweetened condensed milk

2 teaspoons of vanilla extract

1-½ teaspoons of almond extract

40 solid milk chocolate candy drops, unwrapped

A kiss is not always just another kiss; a kiss can please the lips and stomach both. Perhaps you can find some willing female to trade a kiss for a kiss!

Start by preheating the oven to 350 degrees. In a large bowl mix together the coconut, sweetened condensed milk and extracts. Take your time and mix it all up real well. Next cover a cookie sheet with aluminum foil and grease it well with oil. Now place a heaping teaspoon of this mixture on the foil. One spoonful per cookie on the foil. Allow it to bake for ten minutes or until the edges turn brown. Take them out of the oven and place a chocolate kiss in the middle of each cookie. Remove all the cookies from the foil and allow them to cool before indulging!

They say that those who indulge will bulge; well go for it anyhow!

DEVILISH EGGS

6 hard-boiled eggs

1-½ tablespoons of sweet pickle relish

3 tablespoons of mayonnaise

Paprika

The devil in me made me include this timeless recipe. These deviled eggs have been a lifelong favorite of mine, and I know these would be a welcome addition to that romantic picnic basket that you will be packing in the future. Over the years I have seen different variations on this recipe, but I wanted to give you the basics to work with and then you can doll them up any way you want to.

We begin by peeling the eggs and slicing them lengthwise so they look like little boats! Now we take the yolk from the eggs and mash them up with a fork, and then add the relish and mayonnaise with the mashed up yolks. Mix it all up and then fill up the egg halves with the mixture. You can top it off with paprika and refrigerate until you are ready to serve them. One of my favorite alternates is to mix some mustard with the mayo, and then top each egg half with half of a green olive.

These make for a great snack or as an appetizer any time you wish to enjoy something that is "devilishly" good!

Drunken Chicken, Hic!

6 boneless and skinless chicken breasts

1 can of cream of mushroom soup

1 1/3 cups of sour cream

½ cup of cooking sherry

I don't believe that I ever met a chicken that I didn't like, especially on my dinner plate! There must be countless different ways to cook a chicken.

This recipe for chicken is most outstanding and wonderfully easy to prepare. For my non-cooking abilities it was a snap! I can't pass up the opportunity to ask the old question, "do you know why the drunken chicken crossed the road?" Well, I don't know either! It's kind of a catchy title when you think about it, drunken chicken! However you want to booze the chicken up, whiskey, wine or beer is bound to work. The alcohol is a good meat tenderizer and dissolves when it's cooked.

Start with placing the chicken in a lightly greased baking dish. Then mix all the other ingredients together and pour it over the chicken. Slide it in the oven for about an hour at 350 degrees. Bingo, one hour later you have completed the drunken chicken. You might want to consider a glass of wine or two to get the cook ready also! A happy cook makes for a good cook. There are all kinds of possibilities for dishes to go along with this meal. I would recommend that you consider serving rice with this dish and also consider stir-fried vegetables to round it out.

TUMBLEWEEDS

1 package of butterscotch chips

2 tablespoons of peanut butter

12-ounce can of peanuts

4-ounce can of shoestring potatoes

Waxed paper

"Tumbling tumbleweeds", I think that was in a cowboy song way back in the early 1950s or so. Tumbleweeds are usually something you see blowing across the prairie. Basically they are sagebrush that crapped out and when the strong winds come up on the prairie they rip them loose from the ground. Enough of the classroom stuff already, let's get to the cooking!

Start by melting the butterscotch chips and peanut butter together. Once this becomes creamy smooth add the peanuts and shoestring potatoes and drop the mixture by the tablespoon on the wax paper. Allow them to chill and firm up very well before eating.

Kind of looks like a miniature tumbleweed in a way! They certainly taste better than they look, so much for the visual appeal! It's a good thing our lover does not set a great value on visual appeal or we could be in big trouble! The loving and caring is what seems most important to lovers, not just the shallowness of appearance. We could bill ourselves like the tumbleweed cookie, a little rough around the edges, but just as sweet as chocolate!

HEAVENLY STRAWBERRIES

Small basket of strawberries

Magic Shell chocolate ice cream topping

Magic Shell butterscotch ice cream topping

Magic Shell strawberry ice cream topping

Wax paper

This little recipe is virtually foolproof, or I hope so! If you are aware of your lover's preference in ice cream toppings you will be way ahead of the game here, or do all three favors.

From the supermarket buy at least one little basket of ripe strawberries and bring them home where you need to give them a good washing in cold water. Would you believe that this recipe just continues to get simpler as we go?

Clean out one shelf in the fridge so you will have room to chill these little morsels of love. Now put wax paper on a cookie sheet and spread the strawberries out on the wax paper. It is your choice to either remove the stem or leave it on. I prefer to leave the stem on so you have an itty-bitty handle for the strawberry!

Now take the flavored ice cream topping and squirt it on to the strawberries.

I have seen some people hold the strawberries up individually and put the topping on and hold it until the topping shell sets up, your choice of what you want to do. In applying the topping I like to cover about ¾ of the strawberry with the topping to add to the tempting appearance. When you have adequately topped your strawberries place them in the fridge to get a nice chill on them. There are numerous ways you and your lover can consume these little morsels of love. Bon Appetite!

OREOS KISSED WITH CHOCOLATE

1 package of Oreos

1 bag of white chocolate chips

Wax paper

Cookie sheet

Oreos are probably a store bought cookie most of us grew up with. With this recipe the Oreos are just lightly "kissed" with white chocolate for a true taste delight, and they look good to!

The simplest way to approach this fine recipe is to use your microwave and save yourself some work in the kitchen. You can start this little adventure by covering the cookie sheet with wax paper. Then put the bag of white chocolate chips into a bowl and stick them in the microwave and cook them until they melt down without boiling. Then simply dunk half the Oreo cookie into the melted white chocolate and place it in the wax paper to cool and dry.

These are really at their best when they are refrigerated before serving. No doubt they would be a welcome addition to your picnic basket if you were going to pursue any of those romantic recipes that call for packing food with you. These are always nice to nibble on at any time of the day.

Jamaica Me Cool Punch

2 ½ cups of peach nectar

2 cups of orange juice

1 cup of pineapple juice

1-½ cups of light rum

1 cup of club soda

½ cup of granulated sugar

2 teaspoons of grenadine

Here is something very special for those summer days or evenings. This would also be a great addition to your picnic selection of goodies to take with you. From Jamaica to the Caymans, this is sure to please your taste buds and help you set the scene for a romantic interlude.

Just simply combine all the ingredients in a 2-quart container and you can chill it or serve it over ice. This love nectar is guaranteed to get your lover's motor purring. Let the party rev up and get cranking! Just like that old cowboy saying from the movies, "we're burning daylight partner"! Waste no more time and just storm into the kitchen and get cooking! In Jamaica the natives typically say, "don't worry mon, be happy"! The evening will belong to lovers!

Macaroon Kind of Love

7 ounces of flaked coconut

14 ounces of sweetened condensed milk

2 teaspoons vanilla extract

4 squares of unsweetened chocolate

Macaroons are a decadent kind of a thing to snack on. They seem a little lighter on the tummy than other type of cookies. We don't want to overfill ourselves in the process of romantically wooing your lover. This is a rather simply little recipe that's not a lot of work. You begin be preheating the oven to 350 degrees. Now in a large bowl mix up the coconut, sweetened milk, vanilla and shaved chocolate. Careful with the shaving thing, forget your razor and use a grater to shave the chocolate with! For some of us guys this maybe the first opportunity to try and shave chocolate.

Now take a cookie sheet and cover it with aluminum foil and then grease it heavily with shortening. With a teaspoon at a time drop the cookie mixture onto the foil. Do not smash it down, as it bakes it will flatten out all by itself! You could add a cherry on top or sprinkle more chocolate on it. Now bake the cookies for ten minutes or until they are lightly browned around the edges. Remember to remove the cookies right away as they will stick to the foil and be a big mess. Allow them to cool a bit before stacking them on a plate.

That really wasn't to hard, quite simple with wonderful results.

A COFFEE BREAK FOR LOVERS

1/3 cup of ground coffee

1 teaspoon of chocolate extract

½ teaspoon of mint extract

¼ teaspoon of vanilla extract

Even the best of lovers need to take a coffee break now and then! Then why not make it something exotic instead of just regular coffee. A cup of this coffee is something you can linger with and enjoy the luxury that your senses are enjoying.

To get this delightful coffee going, we first combine all three of the extracts together in a cup. Now add the coffee grounds to a blender, ensure you have metal blades in it! Turn the blender on medium and pour in the extracts while the blender is going. Then blend for about ten seconds, and your ready to make a pot of coffee. You can also refrigerate this mixture for another special time if you choose. Could you imagine yourself with your lover in front of the fireplace on a cold winter's evening sipping this heavenly nectar, all the while knowing where this romantic evening is leading. If you need a road map to figure where this is going, then you are not a true romantic at heart. I guess we could always put training wheels on you before you have a sip of this special coffee!

CHERRIES JUBILEE!

16 ounces can of dark sweet cherries

½ cup of sugar

2 tablespoons of cornstarch

1 teaspoon of cinnamon

2 teaspoons of orange extract

½ teaspoon of red food color

6 scoops of vanilla ice cream

½ cup of 151 proof white rum

The richness and freshness that cherries present is a beautiful thing to work with! This recipe is timeless and still pleases all who indulge in great desserts. Won't your lover be amazed when you serve her flaming cherries jubilee! This is guaranteed to please!

Drain the juice from the canned cherries, and save the juice. In a small pan mix the juice, sugar, cornstarch, cinnamon, extract and food coloring. Cook it over a low heat until it comes to a boil, keep cooking and stirring until it is all thickened and becomes clear. Now carefully stir in the cherries and remove from the heat. Place vanilla ice cream in a large serving dish and spoon the warm cherries and liquid mixture over the ice cream. Place about ½ cup of rum on the ice cream and cherries, and then ignite! Once the flames subside, dish it up into serving bowls. With a little extra work you could prepare it all in the individual dishes before setting fire to it! This dish will also light the passionate flame of your lover as it stirs the passion deep within her!

DREAMSICLE PIE

1 package of plain chocolate wafers

¼ cup of melted butter

1 quart of soft vanilla ice cream

1 quart of soft orange sherbet

The name of this special pie can conjure up all kinds of images in my mind. As a child dreamsickle bars were available. Now I don't think they make them, but this is what spawned this pie recipe.

Start with simply crushing the chocolate wafers in a blender. Also set aside about 1 tablespoon of the crushed wafers for the top. Press the ground up wafers into a 9-inch pie pan, around the sides and bottom. Now spread half of the vanilla ice cream on to the crust and go ahead and spread the sherbet over the ice cream. Looking good! Spread the remaining ice cream on top of the sherbet. Now sprinkle those leftover wafer crumbs over the top. Put a cover on the pie and freeze it!

How wonderfully simple, this is something I can actually do and it turns out just great! This is truly a blast from the past, and ice cream blast that is! The Dreamsickle Pie is sure to melt your heart and the heart of your lover.

HEAVENLY AMBROSIA

1 cup of graham cracker crumbs

¼ cup of melted margarine

1 cup of crushed pineapple

1 package of orange flavored gelatin

1 cup of hot water

1 cup of sour cream

¼ teaspoon of vanilla extract

1 cup of diced orange sections

½ cup of flaked coconut

The mere thought of ambrosia in any form holds the promise of something very magical and wonderful. A serving of this magical dish is sure to nearly make you euphoric from the experience!

Start with mixing up the crumbs and the margarine. Make sure you set aside a third of a cup of crumbs for the top. Now press this mixture into an 8"x8" baking dish. Go ahead and drain the pineapple and set the juice aside. Dissolve gelatin and sugar in the hot water and stir in the pineapple juice. Allow it to chill until it partially sets. Add the sour cream and vanilla extract and whip it until it is fluffy. Now mix in the pineapple, oranges and coconut and pour this mixture into the baking dish on top of the crumbs. This is where you add the leftover crumbs and sprinkle them over the top. Slide the dish into the fridge to get a good chill on the whole thing. When you go to serve it, place maraschino cherries on top of each serving to bring this whole creation together.

Now just enjoy the special magic that this dish offers!

AMARETTO DELIGHT!

2 cups of chocolate wafer cookie crumbs

½ cup of slivered almonds

½ cup of margarine

6 ounces of butterscotch chips

14 ounces of sweetened condensed milk

16 ounces of sour cream

1/3 cup of amaretto liqueur

1 cup of whipped cream, whipped

Amaretto puts a nice spin on this recipe for a summertime treat. We need to treat ourselves more frequently during the hot summertime and we owe it to ourselves! Think of how nice it would be to curl up on the couch with your honey bunny and enjoy this wonderful dish.

We can begin this one by mixing together the crumbs, almonds and the margarine. Now set aside 1 ½ cups of this crumb mix for later. Go ahead and press the remaining mixture into a 9-inch springform pan. In a small saucepan melt the chips along with the sweetened condensed milk. In a separate bowl mix up the sour cream and amaretto, then stir in the butterscotch mixture. Mix in the whipped cream and pour half the amaretto mix over the prepared crust. Top it with that a of crumbs you set aside. Add the remaining amaretto mix and sprinkle on the last ½ cup of crumbs. Freeze the whole thing about 6 hours. Now you are ready for your amaretto delight!

CRANBERRY BOG GROG

2 cans of unsweetened pineapple juice

½ cup of lemon juice

2 cups of cranberry juice

1 cup of sugar

2 quarts of ginger ale

Nothing that tastes this good came out of a cranberry bog! This will definitely tingle your taste buds on a hot summer day, or any other time for that fact. Its best served over ice right away. If you let it set to long the ginger ale will go flat on you. It is somewhat surprising that a healthy juice can also taste this awesome! I know that the cranberry producers are marketing their cranberry juice in many ways. The popular thing seems to be for them to mix it with another kind of juice, but it seems to really dilute the taste. It is as simple as mixing all the ingredients together and putting it in the fridge to chill.

I have been told that this mixture also makes for a real good ice cream float.

I believe it's worth a try any old way that you choice to use it, just do it.

This proves that cranberries are good anytime besides just Thanksgiving Day. They are a highly versatile little berry that even is reported to have some medicinal use! I have known people that were told by their doctor to drink cranberry juice to promote healthier kidneys and bladder. I don't know if it really works, but it makes it seem much more healthy to drink!

CHERRY PARFAIT DELIGHT!

1 cup of whipping cream

3 tablespoons of sugar

1 teaspoon of vanilla extract

1 cup of sour cream

1 can of cherry pie filling

The beauty of cherries is that there is so much you can do with them in the kitchen. This is one of those recipes that you can prepare ahead of time and stash it in the fridge for later. Whenever you serve this outstanding dessert you can expect to get a lot of kudos from your lover, and whatever else she may reward your hard work with! Almost everyone I have ever known seems to really like it when someone does something special just for him or her because of their good feelings.

Start with placing the whipping cream in a bowl and whip it, then add the sugar and vanilla to it. Now carefully fold in the sour cream. Place alternating layers of the whipped cream mixture and cherry pie filling in to parfait glasses. Start with a red layer and end with a white layer.

Now just chill it until you are ready to serve it to your little honey bunny.

For an additional touch you could top off each glass with a single cherry or some chopped nuts to give it a more elegant look!

Enjoy, indulge, but don't bulge! You need to hide the calorie counter so you can get maximum enjoyment out of this special dessert!

SOLID GOLD PUNCH

1 can of apricot nectar

1 can of pineapple juice

1 can of thawed frozen lemonade

1 can of thawed frozen orange juice

1-½ quarts of lemon lime pop

This little beauty comes out looking like it is solid gold, liquid that is. This is just a real super drink to serve anytime of the year. Some people like to spike the punch with booze, but that's a personal preference for each individual. This is as simple as mixing all the ingredients together and let it chill in the fridge.

This would be a great little number to take with you on one of those romantic picnics you have been reading about in this book. Something like this served over shaved ice would really please most anyone.

Go ahead and enjoy, who's looking any way? As long as you and your lover are happy, that's what really counts in life. We know that life is short and very predictable, so let's grab the gold ride on this merry-go-round of life!

Just imagine how wonderful life could be if we put as much daily energy into our relationships as we invest in our jobs. There can be nothing better than some solid gold loving tonight!

MUSHROOMING LOVE

Basket of fresh mushrooms

Roll of low fat breakfast sausage

Liquid Italian salad dressing

A long time ago someone told me that mushrooms were an aphrodisiac. True or false, I really don't know, but I know mushrooms are sure tasty little things to eat!

First you need to wash your mushrooms and remove the stems and let them drain until dry. I just love how simple these very tasty recipes can be. Now get out that roll of breakfast sausage and fry it up! Do not make patties; just fry it up until it is cooked thoroughly and crumbly. Drain the sausage well, I prefer to drain and dry it with paper towels to remove the maximum amount of grease. Place the sausage into a bowl and mix in the Italian dressing. Use only enough Italian dressing to just coat the sausage. We don't want it dripping with the dressing, so add a little at a time until we get all the sausage coated.

Now using a spoon, fill the inside of each mushroom with sausage and place them on a serving plate. This dish is designed so you can serve it hot or cold, refrigerate it or nuke it, your choice!

This is great "finger" food to serve along with a glass of wine and spicy conversation.

BACON ROLL-UPS

½ cup of sour cream

½ teaspoon of onion salt

½ pound of cooked and crumbled bacon

8-ounce package of crescent rolls

Bacon has gotten a bad rap as being super high in cholesterol and generally not good for you. Of course it is not good for you if you eat a pound of it at a setting! There isn't anything that's good for you if you don't exercise some moderation. To have a little bacon now and then, like with these bacon roll-ups, shouldn't be any big deal! Bacon is not just for breakfast any more. Its really great any time you serve it up. You can make these up in advance, but I do highly recommend that you serve them fresh out of the oven. Nuthin' says lovin like something from your oven! For your honey to know that you went to all this trouble to bake something special for her will definitely score you some big points!

You can start by mixing together the sour cream, onion salt and crumbled bacon. Once that is done, unroll all the crescents and spread this mixture on them and gently roll the crescent rolls back up. Now place them on a baking sheet in the oven at 375 degrees for twelve minutes. It is incredible how simple a wonderful little recipe like this is to do.

I personally recommend serving these with deviled eggs and a well-chilled summer punch. This is guaranteed to be a most outstanding brunch for just the two of you!

PINEAPPLE BALL

8-ounce package of cream cheese

3 ½ ounces of drained crushed pineapple

2 tablespoons of chopped green pepper

1 teaspoon of seasoning salt

Have you ever heard of a pineapple ball before? They are not for playing with and they don't bounce either! Well, most people have not heard of them either, but they are a great little snack to make. Not only does it taste great, but you can make it up in a jiffy and enjoy it tremendously.

To whip this up you just mix all the ingredients together and shape it into a ball! Pretty darn simply, and it is outstanding if you serve it with Ritz crackers on the side.

This is yet another simple thing to add to your picnic basket to help you enjoy a romantic meal with your lover. Imagine the two of you nibbling on this creation and making plans to take this romantic interlude even further than the picnic! It all sounds good to me! Just simply kick yourself into gear and let it happen!

If nothing is ventured, then you sure cannot expect to gain anything but weight. The kitchen really is not all that much of a scary place to venture into. Go for it and let the magic flow!

Tutti-Frutti Bars Rock

¼ cup of margarine

½ pound of marshmallows

½ teaspoon of vanilla extract

½ cup of chopped candied cherries

½ cup of coarsely chopped pecans

5 ½ ounces of crisp rice cereal

Tutti-frutti rocks! This recipe follows the same line as tutti-frutti ice cream in a way. It is a most yummy thing for your tummy! This is not a hard recipe to follow, and you can whip it up in a snap.

Start with heating the margarine and marshmallows in a double boiler until it is thick and syrupy. Then add the vanilla, cherries and pecans. Put the cereal in a large bowl and pour the marshmallow mixture or the cereal while stirring it briskly. Now press it all into a greased nine-inch pan. Then press extra cherries and nuts into the top of the mixture. Let it stand until firm enough to cut, about one hour.

Tutti-frutti is one of those wonderful things that has been around for-ever and a day. I would not be surprised if those ice cream trucks we see in the summer going through the neighborhood still sell tutti-frutti bars! It's just as simple as I promised it to be. Now enjoy the rewards of your labor!

PORCUPINE MEATBALLS

1-½ pounds of lean ground beef

½ cup of minute rice, cooked

Salt & pepper

3 tablespoons of oil

1 can of tomato soup

½ cup of water

This could be a "sticky" situation with porcupine meatballs. The name of this recipe is easy to remember, porcupines always make me think of needles, and I really don't like needles! Overall, I do like these meatballs despite the porcupine name. This is another great possibility for one of those romantic picnic adventures, or just an evening at home and you need something easy to fix.

For this gourmet adventure we begin by mixing the rice, ground beef, salt and pepper together. Now roll this mixture into two-inch balls and brown them in a skillet with hot oil. Once browned, pour the tomato soup in the skillet and let it simmer covered for about an hour.

Just imagine how you and your sweetie could fill that hour while you are waiting for your balls to cook! Let your imagine run wild and go with the moment.

Snowballs and More Snowballs

6 ounces of semi-sweet chocolate chips

½ cup of canned evaporated milk

1 cup of sifted powered sugar

½ cup of finely chopped walnuts

1 ¼ cup of flaked coconut

These snowballs are guaranteed to melt in your mouth at first taste. Winter, summer or spring, these snowballs will surely delight anyone that you serve them to. This also is a great little addition to your picnic basket if you are planning a romantic picnic.

We start by melting the chocolate chips and combining them with the milk. Remove this mixture from the heat and stir in the powered sugar and walnuts. Allow everything to cool slightly until it just starts to hold its shape. Then place a drop of this chocolate mixture onto a mound of coconut flakes and proceed to roll it in the form of a ball. Now slip it into the fridge so it can set up and get a good chill on it.

Just imagine the delight as you feed a snowball to your lover. The chocolate is sure to please her, and in turn you will be pleased. It is a give and take life we lead!

TRIPLE PEANUT BUTTER THREAT

½ cup of granulated sugar

½ cup of brown sugar

½ cup of shortening

¾ cup of smooth peanut butter

2 tablespoons of light corn syrup

1 tablespoon of milk

½ teaspoon of vanilla extract

1-½ cups of all-purpose flour

½ teaspoon of baking soda

½ cup of chopped roasted peanuts

Just imagine how good this will smell baking in the oven! You might also consider this recipe for one of your picnic adventures found in this book. Just start with a bowl and mix up the shortening, both sugars and the peanut butter, corn syrup, milk and vanilla. In another bowl mix up the salt, baking soda and flour. Now add both of these mixtures together and stir well. Roll the dough into a roll about 1-½ inches thick. Go ahead and chill it about two hours. Now preheat the oven to 350 degrees and start slicing the dough into 1/8 inch slices and put them on an ungreased cookie sheet. Before placing them in the oven smear about ½ a teaspoon of peanut butter on each slice. Go around the edge of each cookie with a fork flatly pressed into the dough. Now generous sprinkle peanuts on top of the slices and gently press them into the dough and then put them in the oven for about 12 minutes.

CHOCOLATE CHIP COOKIES RULE!

1 cup of margarine

1 cup of granulated sugar

1 cup of brown sugar

2 eggs

1 teaspoon of vanilla extract

2 cups of all-purpose flour

1 teaspoon of baking soda

½ teaspoon of salt

2 cups of rolled oats

1 cup of semi-sweet chocolate chips

1 cup of chopped pecans

Yes, chocolate chip cookies rule supreme for as long as I can remember! Start with mixing up the margarine, sugars, eggs and vanilla until fluffy. In another bowl mix the flour, baking soda and salt. Now add this to the fluffy mixture and stir well. Place the oats in a blender and blend it to the texture of a coarse meal. Stir the oats into the dough with the chocolate chips and pecans. Now preheat your oven to 375 degrees and roll the dough into 1" balls and place them on a cookie sheet. Bake about 10 minutes or until browned around the edges.

Now for a glass of milk and a warm cookie, what a truly beautiful comfort food for you and your lover! This will help your little love light shine very brightly!

GOLD BAR CANDY

1 box of vanilla instant pudding mix

1 cup of granulated sugar

2/3 cup of evaporated milk

2 tablespoons of margarine

1 teaspoon of liquid butter flavoring

2/3 cup of chopped pecans

Gold aluminum foil

When is the last time anyone offered you a gold bar? If you're like I am, probably never, but I certainly feel I am worth it. These gold bars are sure to impress anyone who lays their eyes on them, and they will surely want at least one!

Let's jump right in and get started on this fabulous recipe. In a saucepan mix together the vanilla pudding, sugar and milk. Then bring it to a boil for 5 minutes and keep stirring. Set the pan aside and add the margarine and liquid butter flavor. Now pour this all into a large bowl and beat it with an electric mixer for 5 minutes, or until it thickens. At this point add the pecans to the mixture. Now take 2 ice cube trays and lightly butter the inside, and add the candy mixture until each compartment is half full. Go ahead and put the trays in the fridge until the mixture is firm.

Remove the candy from the ice trays and carefully wrap each piece of candy in gold foil. Now you have gold bars to share with your lover. This is another goodie you could add to any of your picnic basket adventures with your lover.

Making Music with Cookies

24 ounces of vanilla flavored almond bark

1 package of cream filled sugar wafer cookies

6 ounces of chocolate flavored almond bark

Wax paper

Making music with cookies does sound rather weird, but we can make it work. Its probably only fair that I say right up front that we are going to make these cookies look like a musical instrument, piano keys! They look really great and taste wonderful, a winning combination for sure.

To get this project rolling, line a cookie sheet, or the countertop with wax paper. Spread out 12 of the cookies then melt the vanilla flavored bark. Once melted spread the almond bark over the cookies leaving the upper left corner of each cookie uncoated. With the remaining 12 cookies do the same thing, but leave the upper right corner uncoated. Allow time for the cookies to cool and the almond bark to set up. Now melt the chocolate flavored almond bark and carefully spread the bark on the uncoated corners of the cookies to form what is known as the "black keys". Make sure you put a good chill on the cookies before eating. To serve, arrange the cookies on a tray so the chocolate keys are touching each other.

Was I right? Musical cookies that almost looks to good to eat! They would make for a late evening rendezvous with your lover a very special and romantic happening!

BUTTERSCOTCH BREAK

1 cup of all-purpose flour

1 cup of quick cooking rolled oats

¾ cup brown sugar

2/3 cup of margarine, melted

½ teaspoon of baking soda

¼ teaspoon of salt

1 cup of butterscotch-flavored chips

2/3 cup of chopped pecans

2/3 cup of butterscotch ice cream topping

2 tablespoons of all-purpose flour

I always look for an opportunity to brake for butterscotch! These great butterscotch bars well melt in your mouth and thrill your taste buds to no end.

To get ready let us preheat the oven to 350 degrees. In a big bowl mix up the flour with the rolled oats, brown sugar, margarine, salt and baking soda. Now grease up a 8 inch square baking pan and put the mixture in there and go ahead an bake for ten minutes. When you take it out of the oven, sprinkle it with baking chips and 1/3 cup of pecans. In a separate bowl mix up the ice cream topping and two tablespoons of flour. Now drizzle this over the butterscotch chips and pecans. Go ahead now and sprinkle the remaining flour mixture and pecans into the baking pan. Bake another 20 minutes. Then let it all cool before cutting into bars. What a great tasting treat for you and your honey!

PECAN SNOWBALLS

1 cup of butter

¼ cup of sugar

2 teaspoons of vanilla flavoring

2 cups of sifted flour

60 pecan halves

3 cups of sifted powered sugar

Snowballs anytime, which is what this recipe offers! I'll bet you never had better tasting snowballs in your life. This recipe will help you think cool during those blazing summer months.

We can start by mixing together the butter, sugar, vanilla and flour to make pastry dough. Pinch off a small amount of the dough and wrap it around a pecan half and pinch it together to seal it. Now place these little balls on an ungreased cookie sheet. Bake at 350 degrees for 10 minutes or until they turn a light golden color. While they are still hot go ahead and roll them in the powered sugar. Let them cool a while and then roll the balls a second time in the powered sugar.

Pretty cool stuff and the best part is that they really do taste good. This will certainly make your taste buds sit up and take notice!

FRESH LIQUID SUNSHINE

1 quart of chilled freshly squeezed orange juice

1 bottle of champagne

Sunshine, we all need sunshine in our lives. This will make for an elegant and refreshing drink that you and your lover can enjoy. This could be a great little pick me up on a hot afternoon, or in the early evening when the sun is about to set. Get out your most romantic self and enjoy!

This recipe is truly fool proof unless you forget to chill everything! Pouring this magic elixir over ice is a real no-no to stay away from. Something light to nibble on is always a welcome edition to this adventure. You may need your strength before this encounter is complete!

Sit back now with your loved one and just enjoy all of the special magical experiences that the evening may bring you! This is the kind of evening that you do not want to rush. Patience is going to be a real plus for you tonight.

Just let those romantic juices flow in your brain, and the evening will come alive for you and your lover!

SUPER DUPER ICE CREAM SANDWICHES

14 ounces of sweetened condensed milk

4 teaspoons of vanilla extract

2 cups whipping cream

¾ cup of chocolate chips

24 chocolate chip cookies

Yes sir, nothing better on a hot summer day that a little cream for a lover's soul. After that afternoon delight you surely deserves a good cooling off! Well, the truth be known, its just darn good at any time to have ice cream.

You will be surprised how easy this comes together.

Just start by mixing the sweetened condensed milk and vanilla. Then slowly mix in the whipped cream and chocolate chips until it is all blended in. Then pour it all into a 2 quart container with a lid and freeze for at least six hours. Now spread out those chocolate chip cookies and put about a ¼ cup scoop of ice cream onto half the cookies. Take the other half of the cookies and place on top the ice cream and gently press down.

Do you remember that old childhood saying? You scream, I scream, we all scream for ice cream! Go for the gusto! I would recommend that you go slowly eating those ice cream sandwiches because those ice cream headaches can bring you right to your knees! It really is best to just linger while you and your lover enjoys the fruits of your labor. You can bet your reward for your effort will not be as cold as ice cream!

S'MORES FOR EVERYONE!

8 Squares of semi-sweet chocolate

Sweetened condensed milk

1 Teaspoon of vanilla extract

Box of graham crackers

Bag of miniature marshmallows

This is an oldie and a real goody! S'mores have been on the American scene for every bit of a half century. Of course the chocolate in them makes for a very appealing treat. Somehow chocolate must soothe something in the female brain!

To start we mix together the chocolate, sweetened condensed milk and vanilla. Microwave this for 2 ½ minutes on high. When you take it out stir the mixture until creamy smooth. Now lay out the graham crackers on the counter and place a tablespoon of the chocolate mixture on each cracker. With great care place the marshmallows on only half of the chocolate-coated crackers. Place the other half of the crackers on top of the marshmallows creating a sandwich look. Place them on a plate and refrigerate until you are ready to enjoy the product of your labor.

These S'Mores would be a great thing to take along with you on one of those romantic picnics. Very simple, but they do have great appeal and a really wonderful taste! I would suggest that you pull out all the stops and shoot for the stars!

BEAN BOATS

2 cans of chili with beans

4 French rolls

¼ cup of melted margarine

½ cup of shredded cheddar cheese

Aluminum foil

Bean boats are way cool. I have always loved beans, but they have not always loved me back. I have always heard that beans are a great source of protein, and then beans are a main dish in some cultures. It is like that little ditty I have heard people sing: Beans, beans, the musical fruit, the more I eat the more I toot". At times I think I can toot myself right into a fog! I think you guys get my drift (bad pun). These bean boats do present very well and look and taste absolutely great! Let's go for the gusto!

First cut the tops off the French rolls and hollow out each roll. Be sure to save the bread you cut out. Brush inside and outside of the rolls with the margarine. Now take and break up into pieces the leftover bread. Mix 1 cup of the bread pieces with the chili and fill up those hollowed out bread boats. Replace the tops of the rolls on the buns and wrap the whole thing in foil. Place these on a cookie sheet and slide them in the oven at 375 degrees for about 25 minutes. Now take them out of the oven and remove the tops and sprinkle the cheese on them. Then put the tops back on the bean boats and serve while it's hot. You might want to consider Gas-X as a side dish! Bad gas will sure take your honey right out of a romantic mood in a hurry!

BBQ Cups

1 pound of lean ground beef

½ cup of barbeque sauce

1 can of refrigerator biscuits

¾ cup of grated cheddar cheese

8 muffin cups

Muffin pan

Barbeque is the undisputed king of the summer time meals, and with good reason. Some people go to great lengths to develop their own barbeque sauce. The homemade barbeque sauce I have tried over the years is so much better than anything you will find in the store.

Simply brown the hamburger in a skillet and drain it well and add the barbeque sauce before setting it all aside. Now take the biscuit dough out and press a portion into each muffin cup, even along the sides. Carefully spoon your cooked mixture into the muffin cups you have prepared. Before you pop the pan into the oven, sprinkle the grated cheese over the tops of the cups. Bake it at about 400 degrees, or just until the dough starts to turn slightly brown.

These are just super fun food treats to make, and even as leftovers they are very tasty. This could make for a great light brunch for you and your lover to enjoy!

INDIAN CORN

1 pound of lean hamburger

1 can of drained corn

½ onion chopped up

1 jar of taco sauce

1 bag of tortilla chips

I don't know exactly for sure if the Indians invented this dish for sure, but I rather doubt it. This little goodie can be a whole meal all by itself! Simple and easy, just the way I like it. As far as the amount of the heat in the taco sauce goes, it is totally up to what you can stand to eat! For me hotter is better, but I know that doesn't work for everyone.

We begin by browning the hamburger and onion in a skillet. Once that is all browned then add the corn and taco sauce and let it simmer about 5 minutes. When you are ready to eat just sit the Indian corn out with a bag of tortilla chips. Now you are ready to let the good times roll. There is no good reason to be shy now, shoot for the moon, even if you miss you will be among the stars!

Don't let romance pass you by. If you don't take up the slack someone else will do it for you! I'm pretty sure you do not want to see that happen in any case, so slip it in gear and go!

JUST PEACHY CARROTS

1 pound of cooked and sliced carrots

1/3 cup of peach preserves

1 tablespoon of melted margarine

Pinch of salt (optional)

Did you know that carrots could be just peachy all by themselves? When growing up many of us were forced to eat all of our vegetables and felt they tasted nasty. Had we been able to enjoy something like these peachy carrots we might have changed our tune in a hurry. We would have probably wondered, "what's up doc"? This is one of those recipes that you can vary quite a bit depending on what fruit preserves you can find in the supermarket.

To stir up this magical dish just mix the carrots, margarine, peach preserves and salt together. Just cook this whole thing over a low heat until the carrots are heated all the way through. If it were any simpler it would probably be against the law to make! This would make for an attractive side dish to any meal you stir up. It would be just perfect with that romantic meal you plan on cooking your loved one!

Beer Biscuits

3 cups of instant biscuit mix

¼ teaspoon of salt

1 teaspoon of sugar

1-½ cups of beer, brew of your choice

2 cans of beer

Beer drinkers alert! This is really something every beer drinker needs to try at least once just to be able to say they experienced it. Unfortunately all the alcohol in the beer cooks out of it! You may find something like a beer taste, but no buzz to it!

To whip up these biscuits just stir all these ingredients together and mix them up real well. Now dig out that muffin pan and grease up the inside with oil or shortening. Pour in the batter to fill the muffin cups 2/3 full. Crank that oven up to 425 degrees and bake these biscuits for 15 minutes or until brown.

Now I know by now you are wondering why are there two cans of beer in this recipe? Well, you are supposed to drink one can while you are cooking in the kitchen, and the second can of beer is to wash the biscuits down with! It would be reasonably good taste to consider these morsels for that picnic you might have coming up in the future.

Also remember that what could be better with beer biscuits that beer itself!

A little dab of margarine and a whisper of a good strawberry jam would also do those biscuits justice!

Fruity Pork Chops

6 pork chops

2 tablespoons of cooking oil

6 small peeled and sliced apples

¼ cup of dried currants

1 tablespoon of lemon juice

1/3 cup of brown sugar

Pinch of salt

Fruity pork chops, sound kind of cool to me! I do have a real preference for sweet things. As you might have guessed that I like my food and women both on the sweet side!

To begin this adventure we brown the pork chops in a skillet. While they are cooking is a good time to use that pinch of salt! Now just place the pork chops into the crock-pot and add all the other ingredients. Turn the crock-pot on low and let it cook for at least 8 hours. These pork chops will be fantastic and present with a slight sweet fruity taste to them! Don't forget to serve the apples along with the pork chops, they will taste great too. A good dish to serve with this would be rice and a glass of chilled sweet red wine!

Happy Mac Salad

1-8 ounce bag of macaroni

½ cup of mayo

1 teaspoon of mustard

6-diced pickles

6 chopped hard-boiled eggs

1 small can of mushroom pieces

4 slices of chopped ham, chopped

1 small bottle of cocktail onions

½ cup of chopped green olives

½ cup of chopped black olives

This is an old trusted friend of mine, a real mealtime staple. Like the name implies, it's a happy, happy food! Just begin with boiling the macaroni until its soft and then drain it and allow it to cool. While you are waiting go ahead and boil the eggs and peel them and then chopped them up into small pieces. Do the same thing with the pickles, ham, green and black olives. Now for the fun part, put all the ingredients in a large bowl and mix them up. It is best to stick it in the fridge and get a good chill on it before serving. This is another great possibility to add to your romantic picnic basket for your date, or a quiet supper at home.

TOAD IN A HOLE

Bread slices

Butter

Eggs

Salt & Pepper

What a unusual name for a recipe! It does have a wonderfully weird sound to the name. This is one of those recipes that have been around for an unknown amount of time. I can personally vouch for more than fifty years!

This does seem to be mainly a breakfast dish, but I'm sure you could use it anytime. A most handy time for this recipe is if your lover has spent the night and you want to cook her breakfast before she leaves! A great way to start her day!

To get started we butter bread slices on both sides and tear a hole in the center of the slice a little larger than the size of an egg yolk. Now place the bread slice in a hot buttered skillet and drop an egg into the hole. Don't forget to salt and pepper to taste! After it cooks on one side for a minute or so, flip it over and cook the other side.

How simple can it get? This is truly a great recipe for a tasty little goodie.

It probably would be best to serve it with some kind of breakfast meat like bacon, ham or sausage on the side. Remember my motto is that breakfast is good anytime of the day or night. I'll bet you can almost smell all this cooking in the kitchen!

SPECTACULAR SWEET CHILI!

1 can of red beans

1 can of lima beans

1 can of kidney beans

½ cup of brown sugar

1 cup of diced onion

1 small can of tomato paste

4 cloves of crushed garlic

2 pounds of lean ground beef

4 tablespoons of chili powder

Large crock-pot

? Nearly every guy I know seems to have developed, or wants to develop their own chili recipe. To put this all together you need to start by frying up the ground beef and draining the grease off real well. We don't want your arteries collapsing while you are eating this chili!

Now for the simple part, just put all the ingredients in a large crock-pot! Turn that big rascal on to cook on a low heat for at least 12 hours. I believe the longer it cooks the better it gets! There are all kinds of good stuff to serve with this chili. Hot bread of some kind really goes most excellent with any chili. What sets this chili recipe off and makes it so very good is that it has a little sweet tang to it! Your honey bunny will certainly enjoy a bowl with you, but don't forget the Beano!

Drunken Pollack

4 Links of Polish sausage

6 Cans of beer, your choice of course!

Crock-pot

Polish or another nationality, almost everyone I know seems to like a good polish sausage. The Polish people have brought some real excellent food to the American culture. It seems to me that a good bit of the Polish food does seem to set a little heavy on my stomach. I prefer it better for supper than for lunch. Trying to go back to work after a heavy lunch can be pretty hard to do. Cooking in a crock-pot sure seems to have a lot of pluses. All you seem to need to do is put food in it with a touch of liquid and let it cook all day while you are somewhere else. When you return your meal is ready for you. I especially like to cook meat in a crock-pot because at the end of the day it is so soft I can cut it with a fork!

This recipe also falls into the category of the no-brainer recipes! Simply start with putting the Polish sausage into the crock-pot and add one can of beer. Let it cook on the low setting for about 8 hours. Now you do have options at this point, you could slice the sausage and put it on a skewers and let it barbecue for 10 minutes or until nicely browned. If you choose you could also substitute with bratwurst or kosher franks.

You could serve these with a wide variety of other dishes. I would personally recommend doing the bean boat recipe with these tasty Polish sausages! By all means follow whatever your stomach commands of you to do! Oh, by the way, don't forget to treat yourself to those other 5 beers that you bought for this recipe!